VENUS DREAMING

A Guide to Women's Dreams & Nightmares

Brenda Mallon

Newleaf

Newleaf
an imprint of
Gill & Macmillan Ltd
Hume Avenue
Park West
Dublin 12
with associated companies throughout the world
www.gillmacmillan.ie

0 7171 3143 2
Print origination by O'K Graphic Design, Dublin
Printed by ColourBooks Ltd, Dublin

The paper used in this book is made from the wood pulp of managed forests.
For every tree felled, at least one tree is planted, thereby renewing natural resources.

A catalogue record is available for this book from the British Library.

1 3 5 4 2

CONTENTS

Dedication

In memory of my mother,
May Mallon, and to my daughter,
Crystal Mallon Kershaw

The publishers are grateful to Faber and Faber for permission to reproduce three lines from the poem Little Gidding' from *Four Quartets* by T.S. Eliot on page 20.

ACKNOWLEDGEMENTS

I am deeply indebted to the hundreds of women who took the time to talk to me about their dreams, who filled in questionnaires and who wrote to me after reading *Women Dreaming*. Without them this book could not have been written. I hope *Venus Dreaming* will stand as my thanks for your honesty, trust and creativity. Thanks also to clients, students and dream group friends who gave good-humoured support as well as valuable insights.

My love and thanks to Styx for being there, especially at Christmas when the deadline for the book ran neck and neck. I made the deadline, he made Christmas! Crystal and Danny helped out in both.

It was my mother who passed on her Celtic appreciation of dreams, and to her go my first and final thanks for introducing me to the vast treasures of the dream world. I hope you too can share its wisdom.

In order to ensure confidentiality, names and identities have been changed throughout the book.

Brenda Mallon
New Year's Day, 2001

Chapter 1

Venus: The Goddess in All Women

The dream cries out to each of us,
Look at this and be attentive, for you must learn from me as best you can.

Artemidorus (2nd century CE)

Venus dreams

Everyone dreams. You may not recall all dreams but, on average, you are likely to dream for about two and a half hours every night. Your dreams tell you about your life now, your past and your future. In turning to the myths and stories of the ancient goddesses, in searching for something meaningful among the sacred traditions of other cultures, women are recognising that the Divine is not only 'out there' but 'in here', inside each one of us, and we can reclaim it.

As well as connecting us to the ancient goddesses, dreams also connect to present-day icons who symbolise women in the new millennium. But how does the earliest Venus still speak to us today? One way is in our dreams. The verb 'to dream' in the Old Testament is *harlam*, which means to make whole or healthy, and this reconnection process is a holistic way to find balance in mind, body and spirit.

Dream-recorder Sarida said:

> They are a nightly dose of sodium pentathol — truth. They guide me; they are beautiful creations, and I value them as much as my eyesight.

In antiquity Venus was venerated, and at that time women had an equal part to play in the spiritual life of their communities. New monotheistic religions, however, had an exclusively male priesthood, and by the Middle Ages the wise woman had metamorphosed into the wicked witch. Women's intuitive understanding of the importance of dreams was hijacked.

Mars and Venus dream differently. Women's dreams are built around intimacy and everyday problems, whereas men's dreams are more concerned with issues of separateness and extending their sphere of influence and power. Men's dreams centre more on their relationships with both sexes about equally. M.F. de Martino, carrying out research in America into the ubiquitous sex differences in dreams, found out that as well as dream content being dissimilar, women's attitudes towards dreaming were quite unlike men's and much more in tune with results from sleep laboratory findings. More women agreed that everyone dreams every night, that most dreams are in colour, that some conscious control of our dreams can take place and that our dreaming 'style' or approach to life is very similar to that of our waking life.

Before we go much further, we need to deal with the fact that these goddesses go by different names according to whether they are Greek or Roman. So, Greek names first, then Roman:

Aphrodite — Venus
Hera — Juno
Athene — Minerva
Artemis — Diana
Hestia — Vesta
Demeter — Ceres.

APHRODITE/VENUS

Venus is the goddess of physical beauty, sexual love and fertility. Known as the 'rose of the sea', she had a mystical beginning. In Botticelli's painting she rises from the sea, on a scallop shell, the symbol of pilgrimage. She rises from sea water, suggestive of amniotic fluid, ready to begin her journey. In the capital city of Rome, not only was she the guardian of honourable marriage, worshipped by the powerful matrons of the city, the mothers of families, she was also the goddess of harlots and ladies of the night. In truth, Venus was regarded as the mother of the whole Roman nation, the mother and the symbol of all aspects of love.

While Venus governs desire and sexuality she has many other facets to her nature. She is Venus Felix, the bringer of good fortune, and Venus Verticordia, protector of female chastity. Of all the goddesses, Venus is the only one who commits adultery, yet as a goddess who is sacred to prostitutes, she is only mildly censured for these 'indiscretions'.

The alchemical sign for copper is the same as the sign for the goddess Venus, because her sacred isle, Cyprus, whose name means 'copper', is such a rich source of the metal. Copper is the magic mirror of divination for Friday, which is Venus' day, and that is why in paintings she is often shown holding a mirror. You may find mirrors in your dreams that make the Venus connection.

Maya said:

> I dreamed my yoga teacher showed me a bust of a goddess standing in the centre of a sideboard in a large and grand house. A week or two later the bust and dream clicked as I was meditating sitting sideways on in my bath, gazing into a mirror. The goddess was me!

It is a shock when you come face to face with your divine nature, as it was for Maya.

The goddess within

Jennifer and Roger Woolger's book, *The Goddess Within*, describes the goddesses of Greek mythology and shows how their stories provide a language of the psyche that is still current today. They tell us a lot about contemporary women's lives. For example, Hera, the wife of Zeus, is the goddess of marriage and worldly power, while Athena is the goddess of wisdom and of the city — she is the career woman out there in the world of business and in higher education. The other four goddesses the Woolgers discuss are Aphrodite, the goddess of love and beauty; Artemis, the sporty outdoor type; Demeter, the earth mother; and Persephone, the psychic/spiritual seeker. As we look in more depth at our dreams we meet these goddesses. Though their names may be foreign to us, what they symbolise is the essence of our lives, whether we live in New York, London or Paris. Other female deities, such as Kwan Yin and Our Lady of Guadeloupe, extend the spiritual and mystical dimension of women's lives and dreams.

So, let us look at the goddesses within us as revealed in our dreams. Usually, one will be actively expressed in dreams, but it is not uncommon for some women to live all six of these goddess roles, although it is more usual to act out only three or four. Throughout her career the singer Madonna has acted out many goddess roles, from 'Like a Virgin' to whore, mother and megastar. As writer Zadie Smith, author of the brilliant novel *White Teeth* said: 'Madonna is an icon — indeed it is written in capitals ICON on her www.madonnafanclub.com website.' Her marriage to film-maker Guy Ritchie had fairy-tale atmosphere, taking place as it did in the remote Highland castle of Skibo, hidden away from the public eye.

Hera/Juno

Hera, the wife of Zeus, is the goddess of marriage and worldly power. She was the queen of the heavens but her unfaithful husband Zeus brought out jealousy and vengeance in her, particularly towards his 'love child', Hercules. She manifests herself as a child, as a fully grown woman and as a woman alone or 'woman of sorrows'. She is the goddess who is most often associated with women in mid-life as we face the passage into old age. Hera represents the all-encompassing life of women.

Athene/Minerva

Athene is the goddess of knowledge, of war for a just cause and of arts for peace. Her wisdom is embodied in serpents, one example of which is the serpent-headed Gorgon. Serpents appear in our dreams, though most of us have no waking contact with them.

Helen said:

> I was in a house, seemed to be under attack; windows shattering, doors banging, wind howling, and there was a snake in the room. I was very scared so I started to climb the stairs to higher rooms, but each one I went into the snake was always there wound, round the leg of a chair or table, then the house started to collapse as if it was an earthquake.

Helen often feels under attack, as her other anxiety dreams about work, family and her broken marriage reveal. Though she climbs higher, as she tries symbolically to work more on a head level, a higher level, rather than a gut level, she cannot escape what follows her. Danger intensifies by the end of the dream, when the house is about to collapse. What does the snake represent for Helen? Which part of her psyche is she trying to avoid? She will only resolve the dream by facing the fear and acknowledging it. In doing so, she should rediscover some of the confidence she had before divorce disrupted her life.

Bushra has this dream:

> There were snakes in the grass that try to bite me and my son. Even though I am terrified of snakes, I am so anxious to protect him that I get bitten instead of him.

Artemis/Diana

Artemis, twin sister of Apollo, represents the sporty outdoor type. She is the Amazon archetype. Boundary-breaking, according to Jungian analyst Nor Hall, she was the virgin goddess who was the guardian of unmarried girls. Goddess of the light of the moon, her silver arrows, like Apollo's golden ones, were sometimes used to punish the guilty. She wore a crown shaped like a new moon to signify her nocturnal rovings as she hunts the night sky. Her favourite animal was the stag, so she is often depicted with stags amid oak woods since oak trees were sacred to Artemis.

DEMETER/CERES

Demeter, recognised by her torch and crown, called Ceres by the Romans, is the earth-mother, lady of the harvest, the wisest of goddesses, guardian of all that grows. In early mythology, in the Roman religion, Ceres was the goddess of vegetation, who gave her name to cereal.

Persephone, Demeter's daughter, was snatched and kidnapped by Pluto, the god of the underworld, as she picked the strange flower, the narcissus. As in many stories, there is capture by monsters of one kind or another — whether from the green-eyed monster of jealousy or the vengeful abductor, there is danger afoot. Demeter called out for her daughter and searched frantically until, finally, Helios, the god of light, told her that the god of the underworld had carried Persephone off to his dark palace. We still know those dark depths here in the new millennium. It is still every mother's nightmare to have her child go missing. Our dreams repeat these archetypal myths. Here she is in Debbie's dream:

> In my most stressful dreams, someone has taken my daughter and I am frantically looking for her. Sometimes I hear her crying, sometimes I just have an awful sense of hopelessness. I also dream of walking naked down the street and trying to hide myself with my hands when I realise I have no clothes on.

She is as vulnerable as Demeter after her daughter was kidnapped. Her naked exposure and desperate search is as heart-wrenching now as it was and ever will be. These anxiety dreams about children are the lot of the goddess-mother in all of us:

> I have anxiety dreams about my children. I dreamt that I sent my child on an errand to a strange place. She never arrived. She was lost and I was filled with remorse.

Just like Demeter, this mother is grief-tricken. In her grief, Demeter failed to care for the earth. All the plants began to die and the people starved. Without the earth-mother there could be no life on earth. Eventually Persephone was released. Before she left that dark prison Pluto persuaded her to eat some pomegranate seeds. When she was finally reunited with her mother there was the eternal question between mother and daughter, what did you eat? Because she ate four seeds of the pomegranate fruit Persephone was condemned to spend four months a year in the underworld, while the remaining eight months she could stay with her mother in the upper world. The myth tells us that while we do have winter when all nature seems dead, yet she sleeps and is never dead. This also connects us to the idea of death and rebirth, which we will return to in Chapter 9.

PERSEPHONE

The story of Persephone, the psychic/spiritual seeker, can be told on another level. It is also the story of vulnerability as a girl moves from childhood to adulthood, where she must leave her mother and stand alone. There are, it seems to say, dangers in crossing that threshold, because you may unleash dark forces that may carry you away. However, later we must learn to become separate; it is hard for the child and it is hard for the mother, as Tina shows:

> A few months after I married and had moved away from home I dreamt that, after crossing a bridge with my mother (with whom I had always been very close), we came to a bridge. I said I would go on alone from there. Then I watched my mother turn and walk away. I felt tremendously sad and, after crossing the bridge, I got down in the shallow water and tried to drown myself. In the following months I suffered terrible anxiety and panic and have had a struggle

> to separate emotionally from my mother. It's as if I am feeling again the fear that a small baby feels when her mother leaves her.

Tina expresses how hard it is to break the bond. We have to grow under the guidance of our mother, then detach from her in order to be women in our right. Some women experience this as rejection, which causes difficulties in later relationships. The daughter sees her mother's attention being taken by her father, and it seems to the child that he has first rights. She sometimes learns that her mother also puts her own interests after those of others within the family or that her mother won't let go.

> A recurring dream which started about a year ago ... It's about my mother. I am asking her to leave my house. I am begging her to go. I point out that she said she would only stay for a short time but she's been there months. She doesn't pay much attention. The rooms are altered and have her stamp on them, and she seems very comfortable. I'm in despair because whatever I say or do makes no difference. Part of me feels sorry for her because she has nowhere else to go, but I definitely don't want her in my house ... The dream always ends with me storming out saying I'm going to look for another house to live in.

Returning to the goddess, when Persephone bent over the one hundred-fold blooming narcissus, a flower she had never seen before, she didn't know that the word *narke*, which gives its name to the flower, meant 'drugged stupor'. Then, overwhelmed by its poison, she unwittingly unleashed the power of hell, Hades, the unconscious, the underworld. This carried her off on a perilous journey where she loses herself and finally regains a new self, as Jungian analyst Nor Hall describes in *The Moon and the Virgin*.

Our dreams tell us when we are going through our own perilous dark nights of the soul. For Ruth it was a series of dreams in which

> I dream I have been buried alive and I'm completely alone.

Jade also had a recurring dream:

> Goliath, from the Biblical story, is pounding up the stairs towards our top-floor flat; his armour is clanking, his breathing is fiery. The only place in the flat with a lock on the door is the kitchen. We rush in there, knowing that the lock on the door with its two rusting screws offers no protection.

In her dream we have the giant, the mighty Goliath, fearsome and unbeatable until the enterprising David came along and slew him with a catapult and stone. The element of threat, of trying to overcome sheer brute power, as Persephone did, continues in present-day dreams. We rerun archetypal myths.

What's next for Jade? She, and her unnamed companion, a helper perhaps, rush away from the noisy presence and go to the kitchen, that traditional home of women, Hestia's centre. In the kitchen women for ages have prepared and cooked, kept the home fire going so that the family is nurtured. But there's a problem here, for while superficially it offers protection, it is a flimsy sort of barrier — the lock is rusted and it no longer has the strength and force it once had. Rushing to the presumed safety of the kitchen just won't work these days. Being in the kitchen won't keep monsters at bay, for you have to face your demons if you are to survive and let your deepest, most authentic self emerge.

Jade's dream may well have revealed the inner dream wisdom that she needed to find a place in her life that was less traditional. When she recognised that her monster, Goliath, was slain by the brave boy, she had a gut feeling that she need not be quite so afraid of the big shots. It isn't size that matters, but finding your courage to outwit the bullies.

In Kerry's dream we see the transformed Persephone. She cannot rely on her mother to sort out the problem. Instead she takes on the adult, protective role to save her brother:

> I was standing on the edge of a lake, on a dock. The entire lake was surrounded by docks. It was very stormy and grey. While I was standing on the dock I noticed a boat in the middle of the lake with my mother and another man on the boat. As I stood, and watched, a man bit into the top of my brother's head and pulled out his brains. I instantly dived into the water to save my brother but couldn't swim because of all the fish in the water. I began to beat the fish in panic.

Fish symbolise fertility, and here they are in their element. There is an aspect of feminine fecundity that blocks her rescue attempt. Perhaps this is a male sacrifice from which she has to be excluded.

Venus and Psyche

Sometimes our best-laid plans go drastically wrong. This happens especially when jealousy or ill-will form the basis of the plan. In one myth, Psyche, a beautiful princess, was often mistaken for the goddess Venus. When this became too much for Venus, she ordered her son Eros, the god of love, to wound Psyche with one of his arrows and arrange it so that she fell in love with a debased outcast or someone equally repellent. However, Eros accidentally wounded himself, looked at Psyche and fell in love with her. After many trials, including a period in the darkness of the underworld, Psyche is finally transformed from a mortal being, marries Eros and is accepted by Venus.

> I dreamed often of a woman I was jealous of. The dream took many guises: being made a fool of, trust being misplaced such as going to the antenatal clinic for or with her only to find the father of the child is my partner.

There are echoes of this myth throughout history and literature. In *Snow White* we meet the jealous stepmother, envious of another's beauty, and, like Snow White, Psyche also had two sisters who do not rescue her. In *Romeo and Juliet*, we have family rivalry and parental opposition to their child's choice of partner. Similarly, the relationship between Jack and Rose in the film *Titanic*, a huge box-office success, portrays the archetypal myth of parental interference when love's arrow strikes the 'wrong' partner. Our dramas are played out in dreams just as they are in cinemas and books.

The following dream has all the qualities of Psyche. The dreamer is chased away from her home, feels abandoned and threatened by an evil, unidentified force. Behind the threat is a demented woman:

> I was on a boat going to this tiny island miles from anywhere. Once here it was raining and depressing and gloomy, and there was someone evil and sick in bed growing bigger and bigger that I had to go and see. The dream changed into trying to keep a demented woman from getting into the house — this mad woman fingering all the windows and doors trying to get in at me.

In our dreams we repeat these age-old fears. In many instances they are present-day settings but the sense of being utterly trapped is still at the centre. Liz recalled:

> I was a in a very untidy room and I knew I had to get out of it. I moved through the door into the next smaller room, looking for a door leading out. Although interconnected, neither room had a door to the outside to let me out or anyone in. I knew I would be all right if I woke up.

Like Psyche, she has no way out. Notice how the room is 'untidy', which tells us that Liz feels something in her life is a mess. She knows if she 'wakes up', pays attention, she will be all right. This dream was the impetus she needed to 'tidy up' her life and to open herself up to other people rather than keep herself locked away.

DIANA: GODDESS OF CHASTITY AND THE HUNT

Frightening chase dreams that leave you breathless have been there since childhood. We are chased not only by people but also by storms, animals, balls of rock — all kinds of things. Yet have you ever considered that those early dreams you had as a child were showing you a blueprint of your life's challenges? Think about them for a minute and consider whether you can see a clue to difficult life situations. What you are running from and how you feel are the key to the interpretation, even though those feelings might have started when you were only six or seven.

On a symbolic level chase dreams may bring you face to face with aspects of yourself that you would rather not see.

> As a child I dreamed almost once a week of being chased by something invisible and experiencing the greatest of all terrors, that of the soul in mortal danger. I always escaped in the nick of time, awaking paralysed with fear and afraid to even close my eyes again. Nowadays the nightmare occurs only rarely and with a great difference; now I know that the invisible monster is my other self; even in the dream I know it's me and much of the terror has gone.

Mandy's dream indicated early on that one crucial issue in her life's journey was to find whatever was needed to save her soul.

Karen Signell, a Jungian analyst, writes in her book, *Dreams: The Wisdom of the Heart*, that being chased by a stranger often represents some new facet of your psyche trying to break through into consciousness. This also applies to dreams of burglars who break into your home, when something or someone is trying to get through to you. We will look in the next chapter at how to understand the deep messages of your dreams, but, for the moment, if you have this type of dream ask yourself what is intruding in your life? What could a chase or break-in represent? What are you trying to keep out of your life? By describing the nature or qualities of the intruder or pursuer, you can discover whether you can safely let him/her in or whether you need to maintain safe boundaries.

The moon and Diana

Pat recalled:

> At the new moon and at the first quarter stage, I dream constantly. I wake up in the morning feeling as though I've been living a separate existence and that I have not slept at all.

Her experience fits in closely with one of the many myths associated with lunar cycles, particularly those about the goddess Diana.

The new crescent moon represents the bow of Diana, a maiden and a warrior. The powerful huntress asserts her individuality and independence by travelling the night skies. Her opposite, the full moon, is seen as the ripe, mature, fertile woman. The waning moon is, variously, the old hag, the crone, the seer or the wise woman, or the witch of old who lived in the moon. She holds the key to mysteries and power. Though centuries old, these images of women still remain with us, just as they have done in many diverse cultures. They live in dreams:

> I am on a journey — this woman had a sister who died but she refused to have the body removed. It was well wrapped up but smelt terrible. She was bedridden — a horrible old crone with an elongated, thin leg and a clawy foot. She insisted on keeping this foot out of bed and in touch with the corpse, which lay on the floor by the bedside. She lost her eye and had a huge, empty eye socket and a dismembered foot, and I had to go in and feed her. She was menacingly evil and revolting and scary — the bed grew bigger and bigger until it filled the room.

The old crone knows the mysteries of life and death and keeps us in touch with that eternal journey. Here, though, horribly disfigured, she maintains her watch over her dead sister, for she knows the importance of the rituals, of sitting with the dead. The dreamer is 'on a journey', and part of her task is to 'feed' her own feminine side, to discover the wisdom of women at each stage of life. As Marion Woodman says in her brilliant book, *Bone: Dying Into Life*, the origins of the word crone are the same as 'crown'. Positively, 'cronedom' can be the crowning point of life where we are able to contemplate what seems so 'scary' in youth.

Among American Indians, the moon is called 'the first woman', and is said to 'sicken' or to be menstruating in the waning period of her cycle. The 28-day menstrual cycle and the lunar cycle are so similar that the link between the two is universal in early religious symbolism and in mythology. Moon cults are menstrual cults; they acknowledge the power of the female cycle. In fact, the words 'moon; and 'menses' derive from the same Latin root.

Nor Hall beautifully describes connections with the moon in our own culture when she writes about the 'Sabbath', the day traditionally associated with religious observance and rest from work. She says the word originally came from *sabbutu*, which means heart rest. It was known as the day of the goddess Ishtar's menstruation, which coincided in Babylonia with the full moon, and originally the Sabbath was observed only once a month, just like periods.

Hestia/Vesta

Hestia was a queen who was courted by Poseidon and Apollo, but was unwilling to marry, and while she took many consorts, the lure of marriage was not for her. Known as the 'shining goddess', she is also the goddess of the hearth and the archetypal old maid. She is symbolised by a living flame, representing the central warmth and light of the home.

Dreams about homes and hearths may be Hestia-inspired.

They certainly connect to a deep longing as Abraham Maslow describes in his 'hierarchy of needs'. Our basic, most fundamental needs as human beings are the needs for shelter, warmth and food. Hestia links us to that, as do our dreams, which we will explore in depth in Chapter 8.

> In my dream, I'm in a lovely big house where I'm trying to secure all the windows and doors to prevent the enemy coming in.

Ella has this dream rarely, but it is usually when everything is going well in her life. However, she always has a sneaking feeling that misfortune will strike. It's a conviction that 'this is too good to last', accompanied by the thought that she isn't worthy of such good times. Many of us are so used to being told that we aren't good enough that we internalise the message and believe it.

Women as prey: pursuit dreams

Pursuit dreams fall into two main groups: in the first we can recognise the pursuer as a person or 'thing'; in the second there is the threat and fear of being chased, but we cannot identify the source of danger. Amanda, like so many of us, has chase dreams:

> I have a recurring dream of being chased by people through streets and vast stretches of land. This always causes me to hide in houses or elsewhere until I am nearly caught, then I start running again but don't know where I am going.

Amanda tries to find a safe place, a refuge, and always escapes but does not know where she is going. In waking life, too, she constantly seeks direction. She shifts from one guru to another, from one fad to the next, each time moving on once the novelty has worn off. Behind that restlessness is the fear that if she stops someone or something will hurt her. Marie is different, though in her dream she is also chased:

> I am in a sinister situation where if I do anything wrong I will be killed by other people who do not know who I really am. If I give away who I am, I will be killed. The dream usually features a chase in which I get lost or can't run fast.

Marie knows her destination but she becomes lost. Added to that is a major problem, which centres on her identity. If she reveals her true self she will die and, what's more, she has to be perfect, for if she 'does anything wrong', that will also carry the ultimate penalty. She is in a very difficult situation — she has to be infallible and not be 'real'. How much of that reflects her chameleon-like waking behaviour? She is always trying to 'fit in' and her true self is repressed. She tries to be the perfect mother, perfect lover, ideal friend and true carer. It's exhausting just thinking about it, so it's hardly surprising that Marie cannot run fast in her dream, but at least she is still moving!

In some dreams the pursuer is vaguely defined as 'the enemy', as a stereotypically evil Nazi or an alien being from outer space. This type of anxiety chase dream reflects generalised worries, prompting us to find an escape route, but first we need to discover what it is that is threatening us, otherwise we may run towards the danger and bring ourselves even more problems. Annabel, who makes a point of using her sleep experiences to help sort out problems, had the following dream:

> I had a machine that turned and chased me in circles. I jumped into space to escape it and then I felt free, without any fear. I awoke with these words going through my head: Now you can start.

Relief flooded through her when she woke up. Suddenly, that Aha! experience hit her and she knew what she had to do.

Annabel, the oldest of five daughters, had taken the major responsibility in caring for her infirm father. She realised that instead of continuing to go round in circles looking after systems that she had set up, and that made more and more demands on her, she could make the jump. She off-loaded equal shares of the responsibility on to her sisters and found some space in which to escape. She had mechanically automatically assumed that as the eldest she had to do everything; symbolically, she had made the slave-driving machine. The dream shows she is ready to start a new phase.

Dreams in which we are being chased but cannot tell by what or whom can be very disturbing. They capture that raw terror of childhood; we experience the dread but are powerless to define or deal with that which threatens our very soul. The two dreams that follow are typical examples:

> I am being chased and am leaving a trail of blood. At the same time there is the sound of a heart thudding and laboured breathing. It terrifies me.

> Each time I get away or out of a locked room I find myself in another one. I'm usually rescuing my brother or sister.

The 'hungry ghost' or *preta* is a Buddhist concept. These creatures live in the same physical realm as we do, but they wander invisible to our eyes as they search for nourishment in a world where there is plenty. But they cannot feed themselves because everything they touch turns to poison. Their insatiable longing symbolises our own unmet yearnings for food, for emotional nourishment or for sustenance to keep us alive. This 'unseen' being figures in many types of dreams:

> I'm pursued by a strange 'being'. I have never seen it but know that it would kill me if it caught me. It would drain my blood away, leaving me zombie-like.

> The 'enemy' is unseen but I can feel them grabbing at me or holding me still so that I cannot move, scream or even open my eyes. Sometimes the unseen enemy is chasing me down

> dark corridors, or places I have never seen.

Some chase dreams can be a way of 'rehearsing' for such an event. Isla finally found her power in this dream:

> I had this recurring dream about an insane murderer chasing me. I always awoke before anything happened, but I was still terrified. In the last dream, which was set in America, I challenged the madman and killed him. I have not had any more of those dreams since then, which is about two years ago.

The fact that this anxiety dream stopped once Isla faced and dealt with her attacker reinforces the argument that, by facing danger, you can develop your own strength and defeat that which threatens you. Many people I have worked with who have had terrifying dreams found relief by talking about and working through them. Frequently the vanquished demons never return. The first step, though, is to accept that your dreams are telling you of worries that you must deal with. Then the success you experience in your dreams spills over into your waking life. Like Isla, you may discover a 'New World', symbolised here by America, when you confront your fear.

Fight or flight: taking control

Suzi also took control and fought back:

> Once I dreamt that my friend and I were in Manchester. We saw the Queen talking to two men. Then the Yorkshire Ripper ran towards her, so we chased him out of Manchester, through a fair, into a forest. Then he turned round and killed my friend, so I grabbed him by the shoulders with my nails and felt such power surging through me. I was angry and scared at the same time, then my nails just cracked and it was agony.

Here, the Queen, the mythical goddess of the past, the symbolic leader, has to be protected. Suzi takes on the challenge, feels the energy pulse through her and, though it is not easy, she is not defeated in her dream.

Our first taste of flying dreams often comes in childhood. Later they develop into two distinct types: in the first, the dreamer takes flight as a means of escape from some sort of danger; in the second, the dreamer takes off for the sheer pleasure and powerful feeling it induces. The following dreams include both aspects:

> I remember trying to run away from someone. I wasn't too scared but they were gaining on me, and I did not want this to happen. I thought that I could gain a lot more speed if I could fly. The next thing I knew I was dressed in a Superman-style outfit and catching criminals. I also remember suddenly losing the ability to fly while high above the clouds. I plummeted down, and I remembered that it's possible to glide on updrafts and pockets of air, and I glided to safety.

Daniella loves her flying dreams. In one she said she resembled a hummingbird that could hover in one spot: 'It was a thrilling phenomenon.' Like those ancient goddesses, she changes form, shape-shifts and experiences new wonders.

Venus in the Underworld

Orpheus, the legendary musician, artist and demi-god, was devastated when his partner Eurydice died after being bitten by a snake. The gods took pity on him in his abject misery and allowed him to travel to the underworld to bring her back, on the one condition that if he looked back at her on the way up to the light she would be lost to him forever. Of course, he did look back, but his fate with women did not end there. His death was equally mythic — he was torn apart by delirious women, the Bacchantes, and his head, still singing, was eventually washed up on the island of Lesbos.

Looking back meant that Eurydice was stuck in the underworld, and, unlike Persephone, there was not even partial freedom. The English word 'respect' comes from the Latin for 'to look back', and to look back is to recognise a dependency. Mothers and babies do it all the time for reassurance and to remain connected to the person they love. As T.S. Eliot puts it:

> The backward look behind the assurance,
> Of recorded history, the backward half-look
> Over the shoulder, towards the primitive terror.

As we move on towards 'enlightenment', we look back see how far we've come and to see how far we still have to go. Myths rehearse our questions about what we want, what is the essence of life and what might be the price, and we have mythic dreams to aid us. Salman Rushdie's 'The Ground Beneath Her Feet' is the story of a modern Indian Orpheus who gets caught in the 'underworlds ' of rock and roll.

Carol's dream at first has a very peaceful, romantic flavour but is also a symbolic trip to the underworld where the consequences might be dire:

> I am myself, in a young girl's body, my own, probably around 15. I am playing with a girl and boy. I recognise the girl, who is on a tyre swing suspended on a huge tree in the garden of a beautiful house ... It is a wonderful, warm summer's day. The sun is bright, the atmosphere carefree and happy. Suddenly I am in the Manor House, which is lofty and traditionally styled with huge oak banisters on a flight of stairs in the east wing. I am being pursued at tremendous speed by an unknown figure. The distance between me and my pursuer is constantly decreasing. I know that if I get to the bottom of the stairs I will be safe because intuition tells me that there is a door into a labyrinth that I can bolt and so lock out my assailant ... The difficulty is that the stairs seem never-ending and I invariably wake up rigid with fear

> at the prospect of being attacked and killed. In the dream I think it will be by stabbing.

The characteristics of a chase dream are here linked with details of a special 'manor house'. At first Carol is happy to be there, but this quickly turns to unease — symbolically, she regresses to a more vulnerable time in adolescence. Carol's 'right brain', her intuitive, creative side, comes to her rescue and she seeks the door of escape. By waking up she doesn't have to face her pursuer. She remains fearful, however, and I'm sure this is because of some unfinished business that continues to cause her anxiety. Also, it seems likely that there is an event that happened when she was 15, or around that age, which holds a clue if only she would consider it. It is not surprising that the stairs seem never-ending, because this earlier event has not yet 'ended', has not yet been resolved. And, unlike a maze, in a labyrinth you can get lost forever.

Dreams, those guardians of sleep, as Freud described them, come from the depths of the unconscious. To know your innermost self you need to 'plumb the depths'. The ancient myths are deep-rooted connections to our history and inheritance. They provide images that feed our soul and creativity, and are the foundation for all we think and feel. In journeying to our own underworld we discover hidden parts of ourselves. The next dream is a powerful example of a mythic journey through darkness and pain, trial by fire and ultimate renewal.

> A few years ago during a period of particular trouble and difficulty, which continued for some years after the dream, I dreamed I was in a large hall. Everywhere was stone; stone walls, ceiling, floor — thick, crudely fashioned slabs of stone for the most part. Everything was utterly devoid of ornamentation. Directly opposite to the raised dais on which I stood, on the lower level were two narrow doorways — no doors — cut out of the stone. As I stood there I looked from one to the other of these openings, and through the left opening I could see a terribly rough and stormy sea.

The waves were huge and threatening, the sky lowering. My heart sank as I looked at it. Turning to look at the other doorway, I glimpsed through it a raging fire with tongues of flame leaping at least twice as high as myself. Beside this door stood an old man dressed in a long robe, bearing a narrow rod in his right hand.

I knew I had to go out of the hall by one of these doorways and was very much afraid. Slowly I descended the right-hand set of shallow steps, thinking I cannot possibly go through the left doorway, that water will sweep me away and I will be lost. I shuddered at the thought of the fire, but chose that, and as I drew level with the old man he looked at me as if he was both sorry for me and yet proud of me for the choice I had made. He said gently, I am sorry, but I will have to burn you. Then he lowered the top of the rod and I saw that a narrow jet of flame was burning very steadily, rather like a gas jet. He applied it to my arm, but I felt no pain and went past him into the heart of the flames, terrified, yet aware that I was passing through them unharmed.

On waking, I pondered this dream for a long time. I was sure it meant that had I gone the way of my own inclinations concerning the grave difficulties that were to continue surrounding me for some time to come, I would indeed have been lost. As it was, against my will yet feeling utterly convinced that I was doing the best thing, I decided on a course that had been recommended to me by my friends on the other side. Though I knew it was a real trial to obey, I knew in my heart it would prove to be the correct one. It is too personal to go into, but I eventually came out beyond the fire.

Other goddesses

There are many other goddesses who hold significance for women living in the twenty-first century. When you have dreams that feel mythic or particularly perplexing or where there are hints towards other cultures, then explore goddess connections. There are many books that will help you interpret your own dreams or sites on the internet devoted to dreams. I have listed some at the back of this book that you can refer to.

SACRED IMAGES

Sacred images of women are universally connected to the image of Mary, mother of Jesus. In the form of the Black Madonna, or Virgin Mary or Our Lady of Guadaloupe, she stands for the sacred energy of women. Dr Bernice Marie-Daly, director of the Institute for Spiritual Development and co-author of *Created in Her Image: Models of the Feminine Divine*, says of Mary: 'She is the only fragment of Goddess energy that we have left in the whole of the West; she is not a Goddess theologically, but in the hearts and minds of millions of people all over the world she is.'

The original meaning of 'virgin' was 'complete within herself', not someone who had never had sexual intercourse. So where is she, the goddess complete within herself? What happened to her? How, like her, can we find completeness within ourselves? The way Dr Daly suggests is by dreaming, using our imagination, being creative, travelling back into history and by 'reclaiming the ancient Goddess figures'. In the next chapter you can learn how to work with your dreams to discover your own goddess connections.

CHAPTER 2

YOUR DREAM JOURNAL

Through dreamwork new areas of communication are opened up within oneself. A filament is shot across the dark gulf between wakefulness and sleep. And then another and again another.

Kathleen Jenks

DREAM JOURNALS

Dreams are a priceless asset that come on-line whenever we sleep. Through dreams our unconscious brings new insights and clarity to help us grow and develop, release blocked-off energy and urge us to greater creativity. Dreams also help us to recognise our own healing potential and our own spirituality. Annette, an avid fan of dreaming, summed up what dreams mean to her:

> They bring me self-knowledge and indicate my strengths and weaknesses. From them I've learned to let go and turn most negatives into positives. I regard them as a mechanism for integrating and healing split-off and hurt parts of myself. I feel I'm on an exciting journey, a thrilling adventure finding out about me. Having said that, there have been bad times, but my dreams are always the light at the end of the tunnel and represent the possibility for acceptance and change and greater self-awareness. I feel I'm a more rounded person in some ways, and yet I also feel I have found many facets — like a beautiful crystal.

DO-IT-YOURSELF DREAM RECORDING

If you want to work on your own dreams, the most important

element is the desire to do so. Once you decide to spend some time on your dreams by trying to recall and record them, then usually you are rewarded by an increase in the number of dreams you remember. This is how to do it yourself:

1. Say to yourself during the day, 'When I wake I am going to remember my dreams.' This is a sort of mental warm-up exercise to get you prepared.
2. Before you go to sleep, put a notepad and pen by the side of the bed so that it is within easy reach. Put the date at the top of a clean page each night when you go to bed. If you prefer, use a tape recorder or dictating machine to record your dream.
3. Whenever you wake up, try to keep hold of any dream that is in your head. In your notebook write down what you recall. If you are in a rush, try writing just key words and then include more details later.
4. Give your dream a title.
5. As soon as you can, reread what you have written and add any details you had omitted. Also include any details from your waking life that you think are relevant to the dream or seem connected to it in any way. Spend time thinking about what the dream means to you. Do some DIY dream work.
6. Add an illustration — drawings can reveal hidden meanings.

Explore the dream

Here are some questions to help you explore the dream:

- Who was in the dream?
- If you were in the dream, were you active or passive?
- What was the main feeling tone?
- Where was the dream set?
- Did anything particularly disturb or impress you about the dream?

> I have found that if I get fussy about which dreams are worth recording, or if I censor dreams, leaving out boring,

> incomprehensible, silly or embarrassing bits, my level of dream recall plummets. I've never really been sure exactly why I do it but whenever I've stopped doing it I always felt as if I'd lost a limb or one of my senses or something.

Later in the day, consider how the dream relates to your waking life. Again some questions to ask yourself:

- Why do you think these dream characters appeared now?
- What do they mean to you?
- How do you feel about the events of the dream?
- Does the dream reflect current waking events or past events?
- Would you like to change your or anyone else's role in the dream? If so, how?
- What is the message of the dream?
- Is this dream linked to other dreams? Can you see similarities with others you have had before?

> I use them as a regular way of contacting part of myself and receiving its guidance. I work through each dream, noting down any connections it makes with what I'm thinking about or doing at that time. I find that just writing and noticing them helps them to work up from my conscious into consciousness. They also integrate with the books I read, or any other therapy I do, and help me see what I might overlook.

A FEW DON'TS

- Don't worry about neatness.
- Don't censor the material.
- Don't think you'll remember it later because it is such a brilliant dream — lots of dreams get lost that way.

> I can dream, wake up, and if it interests me or gives me pleasure, I can go back to sleep and often pick it up and continue the 'story'. In the past I have had long, epic

adventures, cinema-style, which have gone on for nights.

DREAMS AS THE KEY TO SELF-DISCOVERY

> I've found that if I ever ask for a dream to help me to begin something new or make a difficult decision, a dream full of useful imagery will come the following night. I feel very grateful that I still have such a good dream life and feel sure that without it I wouldn't have any common sense at all. Dreams are my balance.

Sleeping helps blend new learning with old. All the time our brains are handling thoughts below the level of conscious awareness. In that way they are like computers. When we sleep it is time for 'off-line processing', when our memory banks tidy up — weighing new and old ideas, discarding outdated information, relabelling files — to enable quicker and easier access to the memory store. A dream we are aware of is possibly just a momentary interception by the conscious mind of material being sorted, scanned and sifted.

> I think it gives our body a chance to rest, but the mind never sleeps. It is like a little computer that has to update and file everything that happens during the day into separate files. The easy things get filed almost immediately, but the things we are not quite sure about, which stay in 'Miscellaneous' until we have had a chance to turn them over, are not filed until we have had that chance. Therefore they crop up in our dreams until we can come to terms and finally find the right file for them.

KEEPING A DREAM JOURNAL

Just in case you are still wondering whether it is worth the effort, here are some comments sent to me by women who took part in my research. Hopefully, they will strengthen your resolve and provide further tips to develop your dream diarist skills.

Zeta: 'I have been recording my dreams for three months now, and during that time my pattern of dreaming has interested me more and more. I used, once, to just accept dreaming as an uncontrollable thing which happened just like breathing. However, I have noted that I dream much more, and more vividly, when I am under stress and there are decisions to be made.'

Trisha: 'When I have trouble remembering my dreams, I write a pledge in my dream diary to the effect that I commit myself to full remembrance of all dreams. Then I sign the pledge. Usually this has the desired effect and I start remembering details again. I wish I had started recording my dreams years ago, but better late than never.'

Amika: 'I recall about two or three dreams a night, sometimes up to ten! My dreams are very important to me, I wouldn't be the same person if I didn't dream a lot. They keep me in touch with my past to a great extent, friends, places that I might otherwise forget. Sometimes I use them as reminders to check up on people I'd forgotten about. They also give me insight into what my worries and desires are, which can be very helpful.'

The influence of the menstrual cycle

Many women find dreams are different according to where they are in their menstrual cycle, and mirror not only moods but levels of creativity. If you have not noticed this yourself, then record your dreams over a period of months, putting a marker next to the dream record that shows where you are in your cycle. You could put P for when you are actually menstruating, O for the time of ovulation and PM for pre-menstrual times. Some women, as you will discover in Chapter 6, also include details of the phases of the moon, because they have found strong links between their menstrual cycle and the lunar cycle. If you record these aspects you will probably find patterns in your dreams of which you were previously unaware, but more of this later.

Dream amplification

Sometimes to get more information from a dream we need to turn up the volume, so to speak, in order to hear the different tunes more readily. This is known as amplification. One way to do this is to ask the dreamer to give a definition to an activity or word that appears in the dream. For instance, Jan told me that she dreamt she was bitten by a dog. This is the dialogue that took place between myself (BM) and Jan (J). It's the 'Imagine I'm from Mars' interview technique.

> BM: 'Pretend I'm from another planet. I've just arrived and although I speak your language there are many things I don't understand. Tell me what "biting" is. What does it mean?'
> J: 'You bite with teeth that are in the mouth of an animal or a person. It lets the animal take food and then to eat it is so it won't starve. If the animal couldn't bite it might die because it couldn't get food.'
> BM: (still as the interviewer from Mars) 'Is biting a good thing?'
> J: 'Sometimes, in the wild, yes, but I'm not food and it hurts me. It should be under control.'
> BM: 'OK, I'm back to being me now. Is there any way in which you feel that you should be "under control"; does anything come to mind? Do you feel that anything is "biting" you or feeding off you?'

Jan could make connections to this. She went on to talk about someone who was giving her a hard time, who was 'dogging' her, always causing problems with her other friends, and there was a lot of 'back biting' going on. The images that arise from dreams and how we feel about them and subsequently interpret them reveal a lot about how we deal with the world, as this one did for Jan.

After using this technique with thousands of people I've found that people's descriptions are very individual. Someone other than

Jan would describe 'biting' quite differently, which would reflect personal aspects of that person's life and her view of the world. We are all different, and our dreams reflect this. We have similar experiences to others who share our culture and speak our language, as well as the whole world, but for all that each one of us is unique and so are the dreams we dream.

Dream drawings

When you draw a dream quite often you include details that you are unaware of until you stand back and look at it, so to speak. The drawings or paintings act as a good record, but keep a journal of waking events too so you can see any links, and don't forget to date your dream pictures.

The colour in your dreams

Keep a note of colours as you go along. If the colour is especially vivid your dream may be trying to draw your attention to a specific aspect. It is useful to do a sketch of a particularly noteworthy dream item and colour it to keep the memory. Leila finds the colours in her dreams have symbolic significance. She says: 'They appear in their cliché context, i.e. red for danger, green for naïveté.'

> I had one frightening dream about a girl with very blue eyes who also wore a blue dress. Her eyes were an unnatural turquoisey-blue, and this seemed to make her look very vulnerable. She was standing outside in the sunshine when suddenly a group of vicious black crows descended and started going for her eyes with their beaks and claws.

Black frequently symbolises dark, evil forces, whereas blue is connected to devotion, loyalty and the infinite. In this dream the 'vulnerable' side, which is out in the open, is under attack. The crows appear from 'out of the blue' and try to take away her sight by attacking her eyes. Leila can work on the dream to find out where she feels there is a threat or what is making her feel exposed at present.

Some women find that the type of colour or level of brightness change according to the type of dream. Whenever she had a warning dream, for instance, a telepathic dream, Celine said it would be black and white or in sepia tones, otherwise her dreams were always in technicolour. (If you want to explore the significance of colour and its symbolic importance you may find my book *Creative Visualization with Colour* helpful.)

> When I remember an interesting dream I feel good all day. When I remember a small dream I feel OK. When I don't remember a dream I feel cheated. Dreams are as much a part of my life as waking experience, so I like to know what I've done and what happened to me during the night, the same as during the day.

Recurring dreams

Recurring dreams keep coming back until you get the message. They are attention-seeking, an assertive 'scratched record' technique that goes over and over the same point until you do something to make it change.

> I found I was gaining fresh insight into the meaning of my dreams as I wrote about them. At times I will have recurring dreams until I 'get the message', and then they stop when I take action or change my behaviour.

> I have found the experience of actually writing down my dreams to be very helpful. Recurrent dreams about work, for example, make me realise just how worried and insecure I am about coping with my promotion and increased responsibilities. Recording and analysing my dreams has helped me get a far better perspective of the problems and worries that confront me and do something on a practical

> level to alleviate the problems, e.g. delegate some of my workload to more junior staff.

Patterns in dreams

When you have a notebook with two or three months of dreams recorded, read through it. See what recurring themes there are, see if there are any patterns, such as dreams at the time of your period or at times of stress. Pick out special images in your dreams, both those you like and those you dislike. You will be startled at the number of dreams you have forgotten all about, and see that reading your own dream diary is like dipping into an adventure story.

You may find themes, symbols, scenarios and places in your dream records. You will begin to notice a pattern and will be able to build up your own unique dictionary of dream symbols. You will also learn which dreams warrant special attention, for instance, warning dreams or diagnostic dreams; then you can react appropriately to your own dream messages. The theme of your dreams will be repeated in some form or other until you actively respond.

> I have repeated themes and patterns. One repeated over a seven-year period was about my car. It was an old Morris Minor, and I used to have a recurring dream that it was stolen. Then I would either find it, or, if in that particular dream I couldn't find it, I would say to myself (in the dream) 'just think hard, Patsy, and wish and it will appear' — and it did! I assume the car was myself and that it was some aspect of myself I was scared of losing or of being stolen and not being able to find it, but that if I really wanted it then it would come back. I would wake up feeling a mixture of fear and then relief.

Allie, a teacher, had the same sort of dream at the end of her school holidays:

> Almost inevitably the night before term starts I dream of going into class with no clothes on or having to go to the toilet in front of my students.

These dreams only happen before she resumes teaching after a break. Once she saw the pattern she realised how anxious she was just before the start of each new term.

Kathee's dream diary shows the development of key themes that are threaded together. Gradually she has come to know what are the most important things she needs to concentrate on in her personal development.

> When I first started keeping a diary it seemed that some images or situations recurred, or rather continued and developed, and others were new, but now it seems that a dream that introduces a new subject or image is rare. It seems more that there are a lot of continuing stories in the dreams that are all interconnected in a kind of network. Some images or situations are more common than others, of course.

Sometimes a theme is repeated at times of change, as it is for Marie:

> I am on a deserted street. I am on one side of the road with a row of buildings behind me. I look over the road to a low wall running parallel with the road into the distance. There is nothing but waste ground on the other side of the wall. The dream leaves me with a sense of panic. I have this dream at times in my life when I am taking a relatively dangerous step. I could be moving, leaving friends, starting a new job, that sort of thing.

Whatever patterns you discover, bear in mind that, as Jung said, each dream is a kind of theatre in which you, the dreamer are the stage, the actors, the setting — in fact, all aspects of the production, including scriptwriter. And, in doing this, we need to acknowledge the negative in ourselves if we are to become 'whole', integrated human beings. By doing this we reown the hidden potential that is present in our dreams. So think about the parts of the dream you don't like, the monster and the villain, and consider that they may represent part of your character. We will go back to this when we look at 'the dark shadow' in Chapter 8.

Big dreams and little dreams

> I think maybe dream activity goes on all the time but the 'I' part of us only becomes aware of it during the time when the body sleeps. I think dreams are one of the few 'doors' to the unconscious mind.

If life is dull, you may find your dreamscape becomes more vivid by way of compensation. The Swiss psychoanalyst Carl Jung thought that dreams frequently acted in a compensatory way, making up for that which was missing in waking life or which was neglected at that time. Most of us have experienced that feeling on waking from a dream that it was a 'big' one, an important, special dream that was highly significant, the kind of dream Jung called 'numinous'. For some people such dreams have been the basis of major life changes, as you will find out later in the book. The other little ones are less immediately impressive and are more often to do with everyday aspects of life, and although they are still very useful for dream work, they often lack the vividness and urgency of numinous dreams.

Build your own symbol dictionary

> I try to keep a card file on the different symbols I dream about so I can see how they develop, and so that I can get more understanding of their often obscure messages.

Dreams are part of the struggle to make sense of our experience, to put our experiences in an emotional context. Each dreamer has her own dream vocabulary made up of personal experience and idiosyncratic symbols. In order to understand them you need to make associations to them, play with them, think about what they mean to you.

Symbols are part of our world language. They hold a profound, simple wisdom that comes to us unbidden, every day of our lives, no matter where we live or what we do. They connect us to the web of humanity that stretches from the past to the future, from the individual to the transpersonal. Our dream images puzzle and fascinate us. We are influenced by the icons advertisers use to sell their products. Images matter to us, yet we don't know why that should be, and certain themes are echoed around the world. We can use that knowledge to help our spiritual, emotional and intuitive self.

> They are revelations of my psychological state, in code form. They tell me where I am now and where I am going, in as much as the present has seeds of the future so they have a prophetic quality. They give me insight into other people, revealing how others feel towards me or how I think they feel.

To build a 'symbol dictionary', write down commonly recurring images/symbols that appear in your dreams. Keep an alphabetical index and include any associations you make to them, as well as any additional information you come across. Here are a few examples to help you with your own compilation.

WATER

Water is a common dream motif. It comes in all forms, as you can see from these examples:

> Dream landscapes are of the ones most familiar with past life style, or of the one feared, or both at once, i.e. rivers, sea —

> I love and enjoy them and visit both in all weathers. Sparkling, warm, alive, exhilarating. Rivers — deep, black, flooded, sinister, drowning, death in dreams. Sea — tidal waves, storms, no escape in dreams. Dreams alert to real danger, i.e. on holiday in the sea was so lovely to watch we climbed down too near until I remembered the dreams of high waves and we moved higher up. Wise as it turned out, as we would have been soaked, if not harmed.

> Dreams that involve me either flying or trying to fly away from danger, and quite often I dream of plunging into deep water, usually the open sea, and I feel myself going down and down (which is perhaps significant as I'm feeling down) and being very aware that I need to get back up as soon as possible.

The quality of the water, the depth, whether it is clear or murky, all provide clues to its symbolic meaning for you. If you dream of this, let your imagination flow in the watery world of emotion, read about it and think about its importance to all animal life and the earth.

CARS AND DRIVING

Cars regularly feature in dreams. They are many-sided symbols that can represent our instincts and drives, our status, our bodies, our technical performance and the view we have of ourselves. In the waking world, a car is variously seen as a form of transport, a status symbol or a means of reflecting the personality of the driver.

These car dreams can be helpful when working with anxiety dreams. It is useful to notice who is driving the car in a dream, and the condition of the car, how the engine is running, whether it is going forward or reversing, and to be alert to any special features it may have. If you have 'car' dreams ask yourself in what ways the car represents you. Julia found this a helpful technique:

> When I dream of a car I know it's about the course my life is taking. Recently, I had a dream in which the car was out of control. I am driving but the brakes have gone. I crash. This is about events in my life at the moment. I do feel out of control, and I'm scared that I'm not on the right path, but I really don't know how to stop.

Just as Julia could recognise what her dream meant, so Linda knew that her dream about driving her car at 600 mph mirrored her over-stressed, frenetic life as a sales representative for a major cosmetic company.

CARS AND RELATIONSHIPS

Isla had a fairly typical car-over-a-cliff dream when she was having problems with her teenage daughter. In it, Wendy, her daughter, is in the driver's seat of a car as it heads over the edge of a high cliff. Isla is unable to help and looks on in pained silence. She does not see the car plunge into the water but wakes herself up to escape the outcome.

When she had this dream Isla had been troubled by Wendy's relationship with a man. There had been family arguments, shouting and veiled threats from both sides, and Isla had concluded that she had to leave Wendy to learn for herself. It was difficult to stand back in that way, but anything else, she felt, would lead to a complete breakdown in their previously sound relationship. The dream shows Isla standing back, observing the action but not intervening. She sees a car that is not being correctly guided but which goes headlong into danger. This exactly mirrors the feelings she has about her daughter's actions: her daughter is trapped inside the dream car, just as she is in the relationship with her lover.

Elaine had a lot of 'car' dreams, including ones in which she found herself in a cul-de-sac bounded by high walls. Those dramatically portrayed her life at the time, as did the dream:

> I was in a car that plunged into water. The car was going under but I managed to escape out of the window, and I swam to safety ... I think this was about a relationship that I did swim safely from.

Her relationship was getting beyond her control, and she just managed to make the break to safety. Prior to this relationship she had easy-going dreams.

Ruby has been having trouble sleeping since she had this dream:

> I was sitting in my friend's car when a man approached and kept taking the keys from me. He then shut me in and drove off. I tried to escape but couldn't. He drove me down an unmade road and we got to a house in the country. Then I was kept in and, though never assaulted, I was terrified and tried to escape. The only windows were six inches high with orange glass and I couldn't get out ... then after a while I was let out to go to work but had to come back every day. He picked me up from the office and I got no freedom.

She woke up crying and shaking, and woke up her flatmate. As a second-year mechanical engineering student, she was finding relationships with men on her course quite threatening and realised she was more distressed than she had recognised. By openly discussing her experiences she was more able to deal with them and overcame her feeling of being trapped.

Let Susie have the last word on cars:

> I have car dreams where I speed and go through red warning lights, and sometimes the car breaks down. I have heard that cars are phallic symbols and may represent the men who drive them. I think this could hold some truth. When I fell out of love with someone I adored, his sports car turned into a child's pedal car in my dream. A pair of his trousers also appeared, faded and full of holes. In a later dream, his car

> appeared as a battered heap, full of dents, broken windows and without wheels.

FOOD FOR THOUGHT

Food nourishes us, and symbolically can represent being fed on spiritual and emotional levels as well as on the physical:

> At the moment I have one type of recurring dream. I'm in a canteen or restaurant, queuing for food. Waiting for a long time and either not getting the kind of food I want or getting nothing at all.

Pauline has been having problems in the last seven months since her husband was made redundant. Financially life has been difficult, and it has put a strain on her relationship. She said:

> I would very much liked to have run away, but I stood by my husband during this awful period ... He's now working. My dreams show me that I am very concerned about the future, over which I don't seem to have very much control.

Life being 'out of control' is symbolically shown in this dream:

> I dreamed I was cooking a dish with four eggs. I had cracked open the top of each egg ready to use, although I wanted to hard-boil them, so this seemed silly. Then I was chopping up the hard-boiled eggs and poured a thick cheesy sauce over them. I went to sit in the lounge with the plate on my knee, and the plate slid off my knee and landed upside down on the carpet. I sat and stared in dismay; my meal was ruined and the carpet in a mess.

At first, Pauline felt that the dream spelled disaster, but on reflection realised that it would be easy enough to make another meal and, although messy, there was nothing on the plate that would leave a stain on the carpet. Just as the situation with her husband had been 'messy' and unsatisfactory for her, it need not leave a permanent mark or 'stain' behind, and the situation can be remedied. Pauline realised that she would have preferred to be 'hard-boiled' about the whole business.

> I also dreamed I was having breakfast in a hotel with my husband and his mother. He told me to hurry up as we had to set off. This annoyed me. When we got outside the door I remarked that it must still be very early as it was still dark. I was still reluctant to go. I didn't know where we were going. When we walked down the drive to the car it had become daylight. The car was a gorgeous, pale blue, very expensive, pre-war convertible. His mother was sat in the front and, as he was putting the luggage on the back seat, I was wondering how best to climb in as there were only two doors. The engine was running and without warning the car started to move off on its own accord up the road. My husband, after a second's amazed pause, ran after it, jumped in and turned it round. He had to drive it round the block to get it back to my side of the road. I watched him turn into the other road but didn't see him again. He didn't come back for me.

Breakfast is the first meal of the day when we break the fast of the night. What is the significance of this meal for Pauline? And what about this trip she doesn't want to make? When you have dreams in which food figures, try to work out what it means for you. After reflecting on the dream, she said:

> My husband is going for an interview for a job in the North of England tomorrow. His mother lives there and we both originated in the North, but I don't want to go back to live there. My husband knows this and I don't think he wants to go back either. I think the very expensive car symbolises the well-paid job that may mean he will be carried away unexpectedly. If this did happen I should not be able to go

> with him immediately, not to live anyway. Whether I would eventually go back North is difficult to say — it would be very much against my wishes and against my better judgement.

'Going back North' would be difficult, and Pauline's dream reflects the ambivalence she feels as well as doubts about her relationship with her mother-in-law. She would have the key position in his life then, and in the dream she gets the dominant seat next to the driver.

The following dreams about food tell us different things. The first one seems a classically Freudian one in that the 'soft mounds' could well describe a woman's breasts, our original source of sustenance. Others reveal frustrations, poor service or being overlooked.

> I often dream about inexplicable, soft mounds of land that dwarf me. I'm eating and it tastes soft in my mouth.

> In my recurring dream I am eating until I burst, or that is how it feels. Certainly there is a general feeling of panic that I am not in control of the situation involving me.

Waking preoccupations influence dreams in which food figures. Laila changed to night shift work and gained two stones in a very short time. You can see from her dream that she is concerned about her weight and eating — she is eating until she bursts.

For Suki, her 'abundance of food' dreams helped her to realise that she needed to eat better, and she started learning to cook so she could feed herself more healthily. Vegetarians may find their dreams echoing concerns about the ethics of meat eating:

> I have dreams about being a vegetarian. I once dreamt that I had a child and was fleeing my own country where I saw men fighting and war in progress. I ran with my baby across

> country, walked by a stream in a wood and came to a house. I needed food/shelter/work and they took me in as a cook. I slightly feared the people in the house as they seemed to be eyeing me up. The cook who was already employed was in the kitchen cooking a large tray of meat, and I knew it was human meat; I knew I was intended to be next.
>
> I have had other meat dreams since becoming a vegetarian. In one a sheep with very human brown eyes was there. I knew he had feelings although he couldn't talk. People were talking about him as if he was not there. I knew he was to be consumed with mint sauce. I can still see his eyes.

Dreams continue to explore what concerns us in our waking life.

Dream groups

We know from research and from personal experience that men tell their dreams less often than women. However, there is no reason why you shouldn't share your dreams with friends, family or lovers, and maybe you'll interest your male counterparts in their dreams.

In America, and less commonly in England, there are dream-sharing groups. These provide an ideal opportunity to develop a deeper understanding of your own dreams and pool ideas about the forgotten language of dreams in symbols, myths and archetypal motifs. Here are some key factors in setting up a dream group with friends:

- Choose a regular place and time where you will be uninterrupted.
- Establish your boundaries and ground rules:
  - — confidentiality — personal information stays within the group;
  - — everyone's dream is valued;
  - — whoever is speaking is listened to without judgemental interruptions;

— when offering ideas about another person's dream, use with the phrase, 'If this were my dream, this is what it would mean to me';
— remember the person who holds the key to the meaning of the dream is the dreamer, so no dogmatic insistence on interpretation;
— the group should be sensitive to, protective of and caring towards each other.

Dream sharing brings people closer together. In the dream group you may find that after a time you begin to dream about similar things — in fact, you may dream of each other and have problem-solving dreams for each other. In years of leading dream groups, I have found that deep bonds develop between members, as much as anything because the safety factor is held to be of paramount importance. After all, sharing a dream means that we risk exposing our most personal and vulnerable sides. As this is the case, 'The dreamer who shares a dream should be in control of the process,' says Montague Ullman in *Working with Dreams*. The dreamer tells the group when to stop, when she wants to explore an image or doesn't want to investigate an idea put forward by another group member. Essentially, the whole aim of a dream-sharing group is to help each other in a supportive, sensitive way to journey in the world of dream wisdom. It is not about telling people what their dreams mean.

Two further useful questions for us to ask ourselves in dream sharing are 'Why this dream?', and 'How does this dream serve my health and wholeness?' Someone in my dream group commented about Suzanne's dreams, 'Your dreams know that the more bizarre they are, the more attention you will pay them.' Llewellyn Vaughan-Lee, who writes about dreams from the Sufi mystical tradition in *Catching the Thread*, says that the very act of sharing a dream in a sympathetic group has great psychological value because the dreamers know their unconscious is being listened to and appreciated.

In a group setting the dream is not only a gift to the dreamer but a gift to the community. What it says about the dreamer's feelings and thoughts touches a chord in other people. We learn from each other and, as we have all been wounded in one way or another, we can become wounded healers.

You can also share your dreams with family and friends. You may discover that doing this helps bring you closer and more able to understand each other. Meg found just that:

> Just recently I've been having recurrent 'insecurity' dreams. I didn't know I felt so insecure. I decided to talk about them with my boyfriend, and it gave us a chance to air the subject before it became a serious problem. My dreams tell me what my mind feels about the way I live my life.

In the next chapter we'll discover how sexuality is an essential aspect of your dream world.

CHAPTER 3

VENUS AND SEXUALITY

In this chapter we will explore the nature of sexuality in dreams. Dreams about sex are normal and pleasurable for many dreamers. Sexual arousal in REM (rapid eye movement) sleep is important because it gets the reproductive system ready for the waking act, a rehearsal to ensure the body is primed for action. Just as dream sleep is crucial for learning and storage of information, so the sexual dimension of dreams has a similar health-promoting function. Even though you may not remember sexual dreams, the evolutionary survival system still operates in your sleep.

Modern sleep laboratory findings show that during REM sleep there is a high degree of sexual arousal, which causes men to have erections and women to experience clitoral swelling. This happens whether you have just had intercourse or are celibate, because our sleep rhythm follows its own pattern regardless. The famous researcher into sexuality, Alfred Kinsey, found dreams can reveal sexual activities not previously experienced in waking life, showing that dreams have a prospective or rehearsal function. They can compensate for the lack of a sexual partner, for instance, if a lover is away, and they identify conflict that is repressed during waking hours. Dreams about sex are also the way our unconscious symbolises our need for union or wholeness.

BECOMING VENUS

Many women are plagued by feelings of self-doubt, that we are not thin enough, beautiful enough or simply not 'good enough' to be desirable. These feelings of sexual inadequacy may be compensated in dreams where we can be Venus, the goddess of love.

> Usually I am worshipped by some hazy hunk that I fancy but I cannot identify him. He makes me feel delicious, mainly because he is such a catch, but also because he spares no effort in giving me pleasure. I wake up mid-orgasm.

> I dream of men admiring me and that I am slim and very good in bed. All the things that most men want, when the fact is I'm overweight and find sex a bit of a bore.

Freya loves her orgasmic dreams. There isn't any set pattern — sometimes the dreams involve strangers or familiar partners — but they are always a turn-on.

> A sexy dream can liven up my sex life. They are important to me because they are often amazingly colourful and I experience nice emotions in them, often to do with loving or being loved. I am in a crowded room and I get a warm feeling because I know a certain man is there. When he approaches me and whispers in my ear and we touch fingers, lips and bodies, I am wishing that we were on our own. We get more and more daring about touching, and usually when it gets to the actual act of making love I wake up.

Early sexual dreams

Early dreams of sexual encounters are often quite direct. Just as boys experience 'wet' dreams before they have had sexual intercourse, so girls may climax during sleep before they have had a waking orgasm. A group of 16-year-old girls training to be nursery nurses told me of their sexual dreams. Lily said:

> My dreams about sex usually start off with someone I know well or vaguely. First there is kissing and then it moves to the bedroom and, once in bed, my dream blanks out to the next morning. I never know what happens.

Her limited sexual experience lacks the 'in bed' details, but the dream reveals her enjoyment so far, and she looks forward to further sexual expression, but not just yet.

There is no specific figure in Lily's dream; she says the undefined 'other' could be someone familiar or fairly anonymous. She doesn't have a steady boyfriend, rather there is a generalised feeling of sexual arousal. Her dream allows the possibility of kissing and even entering the bedroom, but love-making, which traditionally happens behind the closed doors, is blanked out. It is censored as she sleeps:

> I have flirtatious dreams where I am always desirable and desired. If the dream advances too far towards physical contact it's as though a bubble pops and the 'screen' becomes black then goes blank.

These dreams let girls know before the actual experience of sexual intercourse just how wondrous, exciting and fulfilling orgasm can be. They act as a guide to tell them of their sexual development, to prepare them for possible future satisfaction. Such dreams arouse passion, stimulate desire, show ways to sexual fulfilment and, as we saw earlier, prime our sexual organs for healthy functioning.

For Alison there was no such enjoyment. She was exhausted with all the effort involved and the consequences of having sex:

> When I was at school we had a human biology lesson. That night I dreamt I went to bed with three lads and the next day I kept having babies. I just kept having them. As soon as I had one, another would come, and it carried on for ages. It seemed like the same baby over and over again.

Her dream firmly repeats that sex results in babies. There are no 'maybe' clauses to this, so Alison gives birth again and again, just in case there were any doubts — the impact of the biology lesson is clearly taken to heart.

A common phenomenon in women's dreams is where the dreamer finds herself involved with someone she is not attracted to in waking life. These are the opposite of the romantic, idealised variety. It may be that there is no interest or that at a subliminal level you appreciate qualities the person has. Or it may be that you only allow yourself to have 'unsuitable' partners. As ever, it is the dreamer who holds the key to the meaning of her dream. When you dream of being in bed with an ex-partner it may be telling you that you are repeating aspects of the old relationship with a new lover — different name, different body, but possibly the same potential difficulties.

> Being chased by someone but not getting caught and in the end letting them catch you and enjoy it but waking up before the finish. Once I did get to the end with a person in my dream. And sometime after it did happen, and he was the last person, even in my dream, I would have thought of having sex with or even being friends with.

Orgasm

In *Sexual Behaviour in the Human Female* Kinsey noted that women are frequently woken by muscular spasms akin to those of orgasm, and that these are accompanied by increases in vaginal secretions. 'There can be no question', he writes, 'that a female's responses in sleep are typical of those she makes when she is awake.' He found that more than 70 per cent of women of all ages have sexual dreams at some point, with or without orgasm. Under sleep laboratory conditions, we generally censor our dreams, or at least the telling of them, and keep the erotic ones for home!

> Most of my dreams are romantic set-pieces with loads of kissing and touching. I rarely dream about the actual act of intercourse ... I am usually in historical dress, mostly eighteenth century — I'm always in corsets anyway. There are no variations, just straightforward sex. I always enjoy the dream and wake up feeling horny.

Nadia's waking experience of sex is inferior to what happens in her dreams. She said:

> I have never enjoyed sex. I've come to the conclusion that such things can only happen in dreams. Love-making in my dreams is out of this world, and the sensation is totally unknown to me in real life.

In her dreams she has orgasms, but has never done so while awake.

When Julia wakes in a high state of arousal her sleeping partner sometimes gets an unexpected awakening. She said:

> Apart from a couple of times, in my dreams it is always me having sex with my husband, and the experience is absolutely wonderful. In fact, my orgasms must be for real as they are so strong in my dream and sometimes I have woken up and ravished Richard.

Wish-fulfilment

Dreams don't have a conscience, and you can do whatever you want in your private dreamscapes. You have the opportunity to get involved in sexual activity you might blush at in waking life or fulfil your wildest fantasies. Some women really want the sense of being loved and cared for:

> Usually I am melting into the arms of a romantic fantasy lover with the faint promise of actual sex later on. It is the romantic element that is the most important aspect — a feeling that he is strong and powerful and I am willingly succumbing.

Other women want the opportunity to bed partners who would otherwise be unavailable:

> I think the sexual dreams are helpful in that if I fancy

someone I can 'live out' what it would be like to go to bed with them or just be with them, and that usually ends the desire.

Some women find that sex in their dreams is better than in waking life. Justina told me:

> Love-making in dreams is out of this world. They were much more exciting than any waking experience.

After the latest of this dream series, Justina decided to tell her partner about them, and her dreams have now become waking reality.

When passions cool

Dreams can warn you of difficulties in a relationship, as Annie's dream did:

> I dreamt about my boyfriend at that time, who I loved very much, but there was no emotion in that dream, it was as if sex was just to pass the time. Later in real life he finished with me.

The lack of passion alerted Annie to the fact that her relationship had gone stale. Emma's dreams are more dramatic but are still about passions cooling:

> My five-year-old relationship with my boyfriend figures a lot. They are very realistic, full of my deepest worries and anxieties, insecurity, jealousy, which are always justified in the dream events. I dream of him jeering at me while flirting sexually with others. This justifies all my innermost anxieties, and I almost feel relieved, glad and strong upon waking. I 'know' it to be true and have come to terms with it in my dream. My anticipated worries have now actually

> happened, and I emerge from my sleeping hours strong and independent.

Rebecca's dream examples give us a clue to her personality. They indicate unfulfilled desires and failure:

> I am prone to 'real-life' infatuations with men who don't fancy me at all, and in dreams I am equally humiliated. When I do score I tend to wake up just before orgasm. I also dream of masturbating and usually I am seen. Recently, I dreamt that my real-life, semi-impotent boyfriend had a good erection but turned away from me to commence vigorously fucking a piece of white card with a hole in it.

This dream really shocked her. When she woke she realised that her boyfriend would prefer a clean, untouched, unemotional piece of inanimate card to a full emotional relationship. If he has intercourse with a piece of card specially designed for the purpose, then he has no need to consider satisfying anyone else but himself and he can remain distant from his 'lover'. Rebecca's dream warns her to beware of this man who cannot be reciprocal in his relationship with her and who doesn't want what she has to offer.

One of Freud's significant contributions to the understanding of dreams was to remind us that they let us see our innermost desires. Yolanda's dreams chart the process of loss and renewal, and show how her yearning changed over time:

> In 1991 I reluctantly ended a relationship that was really going nowhere. I still loved the person but he was married, and after four years I realised he would never leave his wife. Initially I dreamt about him often, and he would be with his wife and would ignore me. In the dreams I felt bereft, and that feeling was with me when I woke and well on into the day. Gradually, as the years passed the dreams changed, we began to smile at each other and although we could not be

> together we accepted it. Some mornings after dreaming about him I would feel happy and contented that we were friends, and that was enough. Through the changing patterns of dreams I feel my sorrow has been healed.

These dreams show Yolanda's need to protect herself as she struggled with her desires for a man who, ultimately, was unavailable to her.

EROTIC DREAMS

Dreams of intercourse may reflect the act or symbolise the need to become closer, come together with someone or take on the characteristics of the dream lover. Annette has vivid erotic dreams. When she was completing her degree she dreamt of having sex with one of her tutors. In another she dreamt of having sex with both her brothers at the same time, and later she 'had a very erotic and sexual time with a female friend who'd acquired a penis for the purpose of my dream'. All were highly pleasurable.

> I have wonderful dreams of making love with my lover with whom I live. It interests me that I can make love with him quite happily and then fall asleep next to him and dream of our making love. They are warm and loving dreams, and although I find it strange to dream of making love after I've just made love, and dream of my lover as he lies next to me. I think they are important because they keep the good feelings flowing.

Dawn sometimes has dreams of a homosexual nature though she is actively heterosexual:

> I have sex with someone I don't know, wear sexy lacy underwear — I never do this in life.

Her other dreams are usually very erotic or sensual:

> Latest one was soaping a man all over in the bath (a complete stranger, but very attractive and sexy). I was not in the bath but was bending over it as though bathing a baby.

The sensuous touch in dreams arouses our senses. They also allow us to indulge in exotic pursuits we may only have read about or seen in adult-only movies.

> Generally my sexual dreams are about something I've already done with my female or male lover, but there's more fetishism in my dreams. Gloves, shoes, boots, leather, fur, which normally I don't think about. Being in the ultimate sexual atmosphere, satin and fur and a huge bed — doing daring things that I might not have the nerve to do in real life. When I have these dreams I 'nudge' them so they'll go how I want them to go, and I wake myself up so I can have an orgasm awake. Sometimes, I leave the dreams alone to see what will happen, to see if I dream something useful I would like to try, and sometimes there is. But the dreams aren't way out or weird. Sometimes it's sex with a strange woman/man, but they're somehow familiar because they're sort of amalgamations of lovers I've had, with a bit of someone I fancy thrown in.

Dreams of incest

Dreams involving incest may be arousing as well as disturbing. They sometimes re-enact actual sexual events or the fear associated with sex, or symbolise a relationship that is 'incestuous', too close and inappropriate. The fear of incest is recounted by Eloise and others:

> Occasionally I have terrifying dreams about sex with 'taboo' people — parents and children. Once or twice I have dreamt about making love to a woman, including my mother and sister.

Recent and recalled past memories of sexual assaults by relatives figure in many dreams. Some re-enact actual events while others are veiled images. Clare's recurring dreams address the horrific abuse of power that occurs in father–daughter incest, and she has to find some way of working through the trauma. Her father, as she says, has been dead for three years:

> One that stands out is where he sexually assaulted me. The setting was where we live now. He was next to me on the bed and was wearing his usual dressing gown. I was facing the wall and he was behind me. He was smiling and had hold of me tightly by the shoulders, rubbing against me. I was upset and trying to pull away. I half woke up, feeling sexually aroused and confused. In the dream there was the impression that he was not going to penetrate me.

In Post-Traumatic Stress Disorder, these dreams replay the harrowing ordeal, attempting to resolve it, to lay it to rest and finish the 'unfinished business'.

•

Ginette was not physically abused by her father but she has recurring dreams of her father. He is, she says, 'showing interest in me sexually, and I feel that he knows me intimately, too intimately, as he has done all his life'.

> I was sitting with my father and sister. A gold chain which my lover bought me, and which I'd lost in real life, I suddenly discovered in the dream. I had eaten it and it had stuck in my throat, though half of it was still in my mouth. My sister tried to think of a way to ease it out gently but my father grabbed it and yanked it out, tearing the flesh in my mouth ... I was so incensed that I got my sister to pin his arms behind him so that I could punch him. This was an unusual dream in that I don't normally attack him.

In this dream we see a number of images which may be linked to her father's attitude to Ginette's sexuality. Her father rips the lover's token from her mouth in a gesture of violation. There is no compassionate gentleness in his approach. The image of the flesh in her mouth being torn is similar to the tearing of the vagina when rape occurs. On some level Ginette felt that her father was sexually interested in her. Her dreams draw attention to her anxiety. Here, she gets sisterly support and positively vents her anger as she confronts her father.

The sense of horror we feel at having a sexual dream involving a close relative is captured by Abbie. It is full of contradictions:

> In the dream I was at my parents' house and it was night-time. The moon was full. It was hot yet it was snowing, snow lay on the ground. My ex-boyfriend was walking towards me and I felt really happy. We embraced and then made love. The horrific part was, suddenly the man in my arms was not my ex-boyfriend but my father!

Abbie felt sick with shame and guilt when she woke up. She couldn't understand what the dream meant, but felt it was to do with relationships within the family and her own unsuccessful search for a permanent partner. Her mother died tragically when Abbie and her twin sister were just three years old. As Abbie grew up, she came to resemble her mother more and more closely, people saying they were like 'peas in a pod'. When she was 11 or 12, just after she had her first period, Abbie's relationship with her father began to go wrong; it just 'went downhill', leaving Abbie unsure and insecure. Her stepmother was very kind to all the family, but that was not enough to persuade Abbie to stay at home, and she left when she was 18. Since then she's had six or seven short-lived relationships with men who have always been much older. 'All I ever wanted was to find "Mr Right" and be happy,' she told me.

Abbie's dream show how her feelings towards men are closely tied up with her feelings towards her father. Instead of growing up secure in her father's love, and being accepted as a sexually maturing young woman, Abbie felt rejected as her father withdrew from her. Perhaps her father was uncomfortable because she was so like her mother. Perhaps he drew away in order to manage his own confused feelings. Whatever his reasons, the consequence for Abbie is that she seeks to 'recapture' her father in other relationships. Older men who are married or divorced, or at least 'wifeless' as her father was, attract her, but these relationships are unsatisfactory. In the dream the ultimate horror occurs: her dream lover becomes her father, and she recoils.

Abbie has not had the opportunity to grow through those stages of love and of separation from the parent of the opposite sex that are part and parcel of the maturing process. With care, support and understanding she should be able to resolve these difficult issues and accept herself as an independent person who can make a satisfying relationship with another independent person rather than a father substitute.

Not all women are horrified by incestuous dreams. Sometimes women find them satisfying:

> With both my brothers at the same time — it was pleasant and very erotic.

Guilt, glorious guilt

Guilt is anything but glorious, and troubles us even while we sleep. Hester, for instance, suffers intensely if she even considers being unfaithful to her husband, and she is fearful it might happen in dreams:

> I don't dream much about sex because I have a very jealous and possessive husband, so I try not to betray him even in my dreams, which is annoying sometimes. When I do, it usually turns out to be him; the dream lets me see through the way it disguises him. If I do dream about sex, it's usually a let-down.

Hester can only admit to her own sexual feelings if they occur in relation to her sanctioned partner. Accepting that we might feel aroused by a dream lover, or a stranger, does not mean that we have to turn the dream into reality. Instead, we can use the dream to think about related issues. Like fantasy, dreams can provide an outlet for constrained emotions, and Hester could let herself have more freedom, and fun, in her dreams.

Anna does not have the facility to switch off dreams of a sexual nature but is left to squirm guiltily:

> This man/boy had some clothes on. We were screwing but there was no foreplay. As we were screwing I heard someone walking past the open door, and it was my boyfriend. I could feel pleasure but at the same time intense shame and guilt, as well as horror at what I had done. I wanted to stop immediately yet at the same time I was turned on and liked the person. The guilt stops the enjoyment.

The key is probably in the last sentence. I wonder why Anna feels guilty? Is it because she has mixed feelings about sex? Is she not enjoying sex because it is all too quick for her — 'no foreplay'? And then there is the man/boy image: is this how she sees her boyfriend? The powerful 'look at me' element draws Anna's attention to waking conflict, a serious conflict of commitment. There are many opposites in this dream: man/boy, clothed/unclothed, pleasure/guilt, an open door/an act that should be private, wanting to stop/wanting to continue. Opposites in dreams often indicate ambiguousness or conflict. Conflicts in this dream interfere with the full enjoyment of her sexual encounter — what waking conflicts do they symbolise?

Getting caught

Sexual dreams can be literal and symbolic. A dream of being 'caught in the act' may recall a waking event that took place or may symbolise a current anxiety about being 'found out'. The dreamer is always the best person to interpret which one is the most applicable. Being 'caught' gives Bronwyn problems:

> Most of my dreams seem to revolve around guilt, being caught in bed with someone by my mother ... I think these stem from a rather severe upbringing.

Bronwyn feels she will be judged and condemned for her sexual behaviour, and finds it hard to accept her own sexuality because she is still hounded by her mother's message that sex is somehow not acceptable. Her strict childhood enchains her and her dreams highlight her fears.

> I'm always having sex dreams about my husband in exciting rendezvous. A recent one occurred at a medieval fair where I found myself lying alongside of my husband in a grassy hollow with all of the noise and hubbub around us. The fact that we might be discovered only increased our zest and enthusiasm. This is a very typical dream: other situations are crowded trains, rooms etc. Often we are disturbed but carry on regardless. I also have sex with other men I fancy. Sometimes they are faceless to begin with, assuming a personality throughout, or sometimes their identity changes. I go to very great lengths while dreaming to try and have sex with lovely men, but I'm always thwarted and never manage to quite get there. I'm still working on it, though!

Guilty feelings about sex and sexual partners in dreams occur at any age. Ailsa, a 42-year-old mother of three, recalled her dreams:

> When the children were young I dreamt about sex far more than I do now. The other night I dreamt I was with my husband trying to find a room in which to make love. We kept being interrupted, and although very aroused I woke up before a climax. I used to have exhibitionist-type dreams

> — walking naked with a perfect figure, of course, on the beach, wearing revealing clothes. In real life I'm quite the opposite. In the dream I used to make love to strange men and even had one or two lesbian-type dreams, but my husband was always there in the background, and I generally feel guilty about deceiving him, though I have never done so in real life.

Ailsa recognises that part of her would find the idea of another lover quite erotic, though she is shocked when considering it on waking. Again, just because you dream or fantasise about something does not mean that you have to do anything practical to make it a reality. Instead consider whether the 'husband in the background' is literally about someone who does not claim first place — he doesn't come into the 'fore' ground, but is always there for you.

Some women's dreams run exactly contrary to the guilty ones already described, and the chance of being 'found out' adds to the excitement:

> I had a dream where I went away for a weekend and spent a lot of time sleeping with people of both sexes — a sort of communal love-in. Then I went back and told my husband about it.

In this instance, both partners enjoyed the dream.

Rape

Rape dreams reveal fears about male violence. Women suffer rape and sexual assaults, and often feel powerless to prevent attacks; in war situations, rape is another tool in the process of humiliation.

Masochistic or sadistic sexual dreams can be harrowing and may relate to a relationship that is about dominance or submission. In Vivien's dreams she is caught and brutalised by a gang of tramps.

> Walking through a town filled with signs of degeneracy, breakdown — muggers, looters, rapists everywhere on the watch for women alone. I get chased, grabbed at, followed, captured and then caught by a policeman who wants to rape me. He teased me with the fact no one would believe my story as he was a cop. He even came home and hassled me in the house with my mother there. I tried to contact my boyfriend ... eventually he arrived and we all ran off. I was worried about my mother, who couldn't run — eventually she collapsed and I sent her to hospital. My boyfriend and I hid and watched the man come closer. My boyfriend leapt on him with my knife and cut him into tiny blood-stained pieces, then the police car drew up and they saw the bits.

> I dream of people who I am fond of being tortured. With female friends this takes the form of being raped or having an abortion while they are still awake.

In such dreams where coercion, pain and hurt are involved, sex can be a metaphor for domination, bullying and harassment. Jews, Protestants, Catholics, Rastafarians and Muslims — in fact, almost all cultural and religious groups — have taboos about sex, particularly about women and sex. The issue, though, is more likely to be about women and power. Sameera's story, linked to her dreams, is not unusual, though the religious and cultural influences are particular to her background.

Coming to Britain from a different culture, Sameera's parents, when confronted with the sharp contrasts between East and West, felt that the only way to ensure that their children were 'properly' brought up was to be very strict. They built thicker walls to protect their children from unwelcome influences. Far from restricting Sameera, this made her more determined to 'glimpse over the wall', as she put it. She recalled being reproached for having drawn a nude man and woman when she was eight years old. Sameera continued in her attempts to make sense of her upbringing:

> Pressure was placed on us girls not to notice men around us ... I was wracked with guilty feelings and thought I was the 'dirtiest' girl around. Time and maturity have helped to dissipate those negative feelings, but I shall never forget the childhood experiences — or, rather, my subconscious won't let me forget them. My dreams remind me. My dreams of this sort usually involve me being literally raped. I was brought up to be coy around men; even to look up into their faces was regarded as being extremely forward. Therefore, in my dreams, in order to free myself from the blame of promiscuity, the element of rape comes into play. The act itself is sometimes quite explicit, often moving me to orgasm. Always, because it a rape situation, intercourse takes place with our clothes on.

Sameera understands where the guilt stems from and knows that her dreams about rape reflect not a desire to be dominated by men but are a response to childhood experiences. Her dreams provide a sexual outlet without breaking any religious rules. Sameera's situation is by no means unusual, nor is it restricted to her cultural tradition.

The trauma of rape can lead to recurring dreams that are characteristic of Post-Traumatic Stress Disorder. Gina, a 17-year-old girl I taught on an evening course, came to me after a class and said:

> I'd like to talk to you about these awful dreams I have. I feel a bit embarrassed really and don't know where to start.

When all the other students had gone, she told me:

> I dream that I am stripped naked, tied to a big, wooden plank and whipped. A few men come one after another and have intercourse with me. Then I see myself in a block of ice to preserve me. I wake up crying.

Though she was obviously distressed, she wanted to stop the recurring nightmare. I asked her what she thought the dream was about. At first she said she didn't know. Then, when I asked whether she had ever been attacked or abused, she said:

> I try not to think about it. Oh God, I thought I'd forgotten about it.

Like so many distressing events in life, while we may be able to push them to the back of our minds during the day, at night our dreams show there is unfinished, unresolved emotional business that needs attention.

One lunchtime when Gina was 12 years old, a van drew up next to her as she was returning to school. The two men who asked directions then pushed her into the back of the van. What followed were several hours of sadistic torture as they repeatedly beat and raped her. They had wooden shelves and planks in the back of the vehicle, and for most of the terrifying ordeal she was tied down. They eventually dumped her, bleeding and with broken bones, and she staggered back to her school. She doesn't remember much about the ambulance, the stay in hospital or the months that followed, which culminated in a nightmarish court case and the conviction of her attackers.

Her recurring dream sought to rerun the event — whether to find a different ending or to give some meaning to the horror is not clear. But what was certain was that Gina had to find a way of working through the trauma. She told me that her parents had not wanted to talk about it and people seemed to shun her, so not only did she suffer the attack but subsequently felt guilty because people avoided her. Now she has a loving boyfriend and was at the start of what seemed an important relationship. She trusted him enough to tell him the basic story, but she wanted to talk in more depth. Over the next few weeks we met regularly, and Gina gradually exorcised the pain and anger that was evident in her dreams. Three years later, she and Tony are planning to get married. The dreams have stopped; she is no longer frozen 'to preserve her'. Facing the terror had set her free.

Rape and sexual assault leave scars, physical and emotional. Subsequent dreams may not replay the actual event but use symbolic ways to express horror. In this dream the rapist is symbolised as the 'madman' who is a threat to all women:

> I dream about me, my mum and sister walking through the country at night, and a madman is chasing us. I see my mum and sister go to horrible deaths but I always survive or start crying and wake myself up. I also have a nightmare about when I was raped when I was 14, and I always wake up crying or screaming as I was very frightened when it happened, and it still recurs very often. I was baby-sitting and I let some boys in that I knew. I had taken the baby upstairs, they followed me up, and that is when it happened.

Lydia's dreams tell us that she has not got over that trauma and should get help to do so. They also show that part of her died in that assault: her innocence, her freedom to choose, her view of herself as a whole female. In the dream her mother and sister 'go to horrible deaths'; some aspect of herself as symbolised by her sister and mother was destroyed. Lydia could contact a rape crisis line. The women volunteers who take the calls recognise the severe effect rape has on its victims, not only physically but mentally, and know that such scars can last a lifetime. They respond to calls about rape no matter how long ago it happened. It's not too late for Lydia.

Nina also experiences dream violence:

> This man I really like takes me to a hotel room, and we shower together and have a row and a fight. He hits me and becomes overpowering. We then make love.

For Nina, pain is a familiar bad feeling that, in some perverse way, is more 'comfortable' than allowing herself to experience new emotions. She may need the row, the fight and the force in order to let herself go. Perhaps she feels guilty if she willingly enters into sex — this way, she always has the excuse that she didn't want to.

Venus and Lesbos

> Two or three times my dreams have been lesbian in nature, though I am not inclined that way in waking life. The feelings are intense though the details are vague, and they intrigue rather than disturb me.

Dreams about sexual encounters with other women are not uncommon, nor are they confined solely to lesbians or bisexuals. Some 10 per cent of women who took part in my survey for *Women Dreaming* had experienced erotic dreams in which they were with another woman, though heterosexual women often found them quite difficult to discuss. They were uncomfortable admitting that they felt sexually aroused by another woman when in waking life they were aware of sexual attraction only to men.

> I dreamt there was a girl in bed with me and she had her hand on my thigh and she wanted sex. My girl friend was crawling around on the floor looking for something. All I said was: 'No, I can't, she is in the room.' When I looked out of the window, there was a full moon, where it looked like a mouth on that part of the moon, I saw a tongue sticking out of it.

Dreams reveal that we can appreciate sexuality in many more ways than are prescribed by majority social norms. Judith often used to dream she was a lesbian before she 'came out'. Now her sexual dreams are wholly about women, or groups of women, in a 'Rubens-style' landscape. This dream focuses on sensuality:

> I dream repeatedly about an actual situation — the most satisfying sexual experience I have known is recreated, out

> of context. T. makes love to me — sometimes I wake up then, but on other occasions I then make love to her. I am aware mainly of the sense of touching her skin. Also I dream about sex with close women friends, especially a particular couple, sometimes individually or sometimes both at once. I feel guilty if I have dreamt of only one of them as if breaking a taboo or intruding on their relationship. I also dream of sex with women who I like but would not normally feel sexually attracted to. Occasionally I dream of a kind of group sex with women, like in a classical painting — Greek goddesses etc. in a landscape.

The sensuous quality of the dream does not rely on genital contact but on the exquisite experience of touching her lover's skin. Rose, however, wants genital contact, and in her very erotic dreams about her friend Denise, she finds that Denise 'has conveniently grown a penis'.

Lesbians sometimes find that their struggle in a society that marginalises them may surface in dreams, as in Honor's case:

> In my dream there was an overall feeling of love and warmth at first. Elizabeth, my lover, was there and, although I wasn't touching her, I felt that she was caressing me and that I was close to her. Everything around her was red and warm. But suddenly a huge crowd of people came between us, all very active and noisy; work colleagues, my daughter and her two friends, and my husband. All were unaware of me. Suddenly, I was naked, running, breathless and frightened; in the distance was a car I needed to get to. However hard I ran, I couldn't get any nearer, and I had a terrific sense of panic. I could still see Elizabeth but now, however hard I tried to attract her attention, she only looked at everyone else ... I was screaming her name. Then my husband was bending over me telling me he loved me and beginning to make love to me. I felt a great weight bearing down on me, everything was dark and hot. I could hear what he was saying, but I

could only think of her. As his body bent over me, it was her hands, her kisses and her eyes that I saw. I felt I had lost her and was mourning for all the other loves I've hidden and lost.

Such a graphic dream tells its own story. Honor, married to a kind, considerate man for twenty-two years, left home last year to live with a woman. At 44, she felt she had to acknowledge the lesbianism that she had fought against for years. Her son of 19 and daughter of 20 found it difficult to accept the situation. The dream shows the obstacles she faced and her desperation and powerlessness. She grieves for the time she has lost and the loves that went unspoken.

Louise gained a lot of insight into her own sexuality when she spent time working on her dreams. Parts were easily understood but others left her puzzled:

> The sexual dreams I do have are bizarre: being made love to by a young, punk girl; or by female, old school friends; masturbating in front of people, and so on. Generally in these sexual dreams I feel uncomfortable, embarrassed and, almost, that I don't have the right to pleasure. I am noticeably passive.

Louise knew there were other more confrontational dreams, which she chose to forget. She is grappling with guilt at being active and guilt at being happy.

Dreading the possibility of her early twenties' dreams becoming reality, Lucy, now an advertising rep for a large London agency, fought to suppress it:

> I was kissing a close female friend and we were telling each other that it was all right. At the time it disturbed me very much and I broke off our friendship, although now I have accepted the fact of my lesbianism.

Lucy knew that this 'big' dream had particular importance for her, though at the time she was unable to deal with it. Many women have had similar erotic dreams about female friends but are not moved to end their relationships — instead they accept that they are subconsciously acknowledging those friends' attractiveness. Lucy realised later that she had been trying to repress her true sexual orientation for years.

Famous and infamous

Myth has it that women dream about royalty or media heroes all the time. Closer to the truth is that approximately 6 per cent of women dream about famous people, and there is usually an element of surprise, as there is in this dream of Cleo's:

> I was told by a woman that I had to seduce Hitler and then kill him. I had seduced him and was sitting on him; he was also sitting upright. He had just entered me when a woman walked behind him and handed me a pair of scissors. I stabbed him in his back. I was thinking, what an awful thing to do at a time like this. I was actually enjoying the feeling of him inside me, but I told myself he was a bad, evil man who deserved to die, and I shouldn't be enjoying it.

Cleo has a conflict on her hands: there is someone hateful with whom she is intimately involved whom she needs to destroy, but part of her enjoys and desires the involvement. There is something going on in the background, behind his back, as shown in the scissors being handed to Cleo behind 'Hitler's' back, and she stabs him 'in the back'. She can radically change things if she wants to. That another woman hands her the death implement probably means that the dream symbolism relates to her femaleness. Cleo's strength as a woman is doubled by this accomplice, for she needs additional female power if she is to accomplish her task. This does not necessarily mean another female to help her, but that there is a stronger, more determined, possibly more ruthless part of herself that is available to her should she acknowledge it. The dream tells her she can activate that power.

This dream mirrors Cleo's relationship, which she recognises as being very bad for her. Her dreaming mind uses an ultimate image of evil in 'Hitler'. She finds it hard to resist the sexual pleasure despite her knowledge of the danger involved. As in addiction, the thing we love the most has the power to kill us.

There is wish-fulfilment in Ruby's dream:

> I meet a film star I really like who takes me out for a meal. I am usually about 25 in my dreams, though I am 16 in reality. And, after seeing him for a while, our relationship gets closer and closer, and we end up making love. Afterwards we sleep in each other's arms and then, as he is about to wake me, I am woken up by my mum, so I never know what happens.

These dream lovers give access to the unattainable. In our dreams we can all be adored goddesses. Perhaps Gloria's dream is also about wish-fulfilment, but it is of a much more lusty, phallic-centred variety:

> The Grand Old Duke of York — I have never seen him — was sitting in a caravan in a circus ground. He had a huge penis stretching to the other end of the caravan. I can't remember the rest but I woke up feeling excited.

Gloria adds that she usually dreams about sex when she is feeling sexually frustrated. Is this the Grand Old Duke of York who marched up to the top of the hill and down to the bottom; up again and down again? Interesting, isn't it, how this movement is associated with the act of intercourse? Certainly Freudian interpretation would consider it so. The caravan and circus ground may be symbols of impermanence, but they are exciting places where anything can happen.

Unusual developments

Also there are androgenous individuals who incorporate both masculinity and femininity into themselves. Some women find that they develop male characteristics in dreams, which can be shocking, as Amy found:

> I once had a dream where I had a penis — I found it horrendous, not at all sexy.

Amy preferred her 'romantic set-piece' dreams, which did not include intercourse. Her strong reaction to the dream is important. Other women might have found the idea odd, or amusing, or even something of an adventure, but Amy hates it. A penis typically symbolises masculinity and power, and Amy may find it hard to acknowledge the parts of her personality traditionally attributed to the masculine, such as her strength, her aggressiveness and her anger. We are all made up of masculine and feminine attributes, and need to find the balance between them. Amy's unconscious is determined to make her recognise her full potential, though, because her dream has revealed her masculinity in the most direct way possible.

The following dream shows a completely integrated male and female aspect. Unlike Amy, Catriona has no sense of horror:

> I dreamt I was both a male and myself, and I was making love to myself. We made love at a kitchen table and it made everyone late waiting on us.

Toni, a copywriter working in Edinburgh, also has a bizarre dream that includes a penis:

> I very often dream of babies so small they are like dolls made out of clothes pegs. The 'toy' doll becomes a penis, and I squeeze sperm out of it like toothpaste, then I breastfeed it. Then it is back as a baby.

This dream describes a cycle of sexual reproduction, though the female genitals are omitted. First there is the 'toy' baby doll, then the penis from which comes sperm. The penis is breastfed and in turn becomes a baby. What is the woman's part in all this? She is the 'servicer'; she gets the sperm out of the penis by squeezing it, not through intercourse, and she feeds it with breast milk. Nowhere is sexual pleasure of importance. The whole dream has an atmosphere of wooden matter-of-factness; there is no emotion, merely tasks to perform. She is trapped in the cycle.

Toni provided further details of her sleeping life:

> In one dream I had to make love to a very thin Filipino out of pity. I felt guilty committing adultery, but very worried when he told me he had got VD and showed me a scratch which proved it. Then someone else told me he was tubercular. I did not think I could catch that, but I was angry at his deception. I think this dream was set in a hotel room abroad.

A hotel room abroad is distant and foreign, but as the setting for the dream it may tell us more about Toni. She is keeping away from the tricky sex issues that emerge in her dreams. Again we see her engaged in something she is not personally interested in. She is having sex because she pities this man — there is the 'foreign' element. Then she discovers he is diseased; he can infect her because she makes herself open and vulnerable. Again she is in the servicer role. She is as uncaring about her own well-being as the 'takers' are. At the end of the dream she is angry at the man's deception, but we are not left with the feeling that she is going to do anything about it. In her passive acceptance she gives away her power. She appears to be caught in a cycle with 'unreal' people who give her nothing.

Sexual dysfunction — how can dreams help?

As a last point before we leave sexuality and dreams, as noted at the beginning of the chapter, every night we go through the rhythm of REM sleep and sexual arousal. However, where someone is suffering from sexual dysfunction this pattern may be absent. A couple of nights in a sleep laboratory will help to diagnose whether the difficulty is a physical one, in which case the sexual changes in the genitals will be absent, or a psychological one, in which case there will be clitoral engorgement in women or erection in men. If this is a problem for you, get a referral to a sleep clinic where you can get expert help.

The diversity of sexual dreams is echoed in dreams about many types of relationships. In the next chapter we will explore the way dreams inform us about family and colleagues, friends and enemies, and how they act as guides in times of change.

Chapter 4

The Company She Keeps

Every woman extends backwards into her mother and forwards into her daughter.

Carl Jung

Family, friends and enemies appear in our dream dramas, as do neighbours and colleagues. The company we keep inhabit our dreams just as they do in our waking life, but below the surface we may know a lot more about these relationships than we think we do.

The Great Mother goddess

The Great Mother goddess can be the good mother who gives food and nurtures her child, or she can be the devouring, seductive and destructive mother who causes fear and 'a desire for revenge' in her child. We see this dual, love–hate aspect of the mother–daughter relationship in dreams. The archetypal 'Mother Goddess' figure is still with us, just as she was in Neolithic times when the rounded Venus of Wallendorf was carved out of stone, a symbol of fertility and strength. We meet her once more in our dreams.

From an early age Kay has had a difficult relationship with her mother. After her mother broke her spine in an accident, she was confined to a wheelchair, and this meant that roles were often reversed. Kay became the chief carer and her mother the rebellious dependant. Kay's dreams reflected their dysfunctional relationship. One night Kay dreamt that her mother pointed to her wheelchair and screamed: 'You did this. I'll get you!' 'All the time she was pushing herself nearer and nearer to me,' Kay said. In the dream the wheelchair was a threatening weapon.

After a period of estrangement Kay was trying to renew the contact, then she had another dream, set in the avenue where Kay now lives. She dreamt her mother was running after her with a knife, shouting at her.

> My dream was really telling me to forget trying to find my mother, but I still went to my mother's old address. I traced her through the Salvation Army but she didn't want to have anything to do with me, so I have left it at that. But this dream has really told me to keep away from my mother and to accept the fact that she is ill. It's painful, but I accept now that it's true.

Although they no longer live together, the mother's fearful power is still apparent. On considering the latter dream, Kay told me:

> Looking back at it, it does make sense. Quite a long time before I had the dream, a solicitor told me not to go near my mother, as she might go for me with a knife, but I didn't listen.

Mother–daughter relationships

Full of love or fraught with difficulties, the mother–daughter relationship features strongly in our dreams. We forge the first, closest physical bond to our mother. She carries us for nine months then releases us into the world. The relationship girls have with their mothers is supremely important for emotional development. In that relationship we learn how to be women, discover what is acceptable for girls to be and learn about the roles women and men play.

Mothers fear for their children and so may be overprotective. This is clear for Amber:

> I dreamt of strangling my mother. I think it was because I felt suppressed by her and couldn't tell her what I felt.

Other relationships within the family, for instance, between mothers and brothers, or mother and father, can raise fears that there is not enough love to go round, so we feel left out. This may lead to withdrawal on the part of the girl-child and later the woman. She will keep part of herself back in case she has a rival for any relationship in which she has a great investment. This 'recurring, stressful' theme upsets Ursula:

> My dreams are always of my mother, and they are always of the same type. For some unknown or trivial reason she is very antagonistic, verbally hurtful, demoralising and disparaging towards me. In one particular dream I was sobbing because she told me that she had never really loved me, although she was deeply upset at my elder sister leaving home to get married, because she missed her badly. I have four sisters, and in some of these dreams one or other of them is deliberately provoking my mother to be even nastier. I am puzzled by these dreams ... but according to the rest of the family I am more like my mother in personality than any of them. Maybe there are parts of my mother's personality in me that she doesn't want to be reminded of.

Ursula's dreams throw up a number of conflicts frequently found in the mother–daughter relationship. She still needs her mother's love intensely yet fears unprovoked attacks. Somehow she will have to address the distress that lies below the surface. Though she felt she and her mother and sisters have 'a very good, close relationship', her dreams indicate that there is something amiss that could be dealt with.

Hilary rarely dreams of her mother:

> The last one was set back in time. I was in a hospital. My mother was a nurse trying to save my life, but I died.

Here the mother is a helpful, caring person who, though she tries, cannot save Hilary. Maybe she doesn't have the power. Maybe

Hilary was going to die anyway and no one could have done any better. Whatever the reason, the mother was unable to protect her.

Frequently, in dreams, death means change: the change from one part of life to another, the change from childhood to adulthood, perhaps the change from an unsatisfying way of life to a more satisfactory one. In the transition from being a dependant child to becoming an autonomous individual, one of the most painful realisations is that our parents are not all-powerful and cannot protect us from the big wide world and all its tribulations. The dream could be helping Hilary to come to terms with this. Growing up is a painful process, whatever the age at which we do it.

Consider also, should you have a dream like Keeley's, whether the words are significant. They usually are:

> I have recurring dreams of being smothered or strangled. Sometimes I drown. These dreams tell me who to avoid. In one my mother was suffocating me. She frightens me in real life.

Keeley found it difficult to break away from her overprotective and domineering mother. A longing for maternal love can be displaced in dreams that act as some form of compensation, as it does for the next dreamer:

> I dream about babies because I want one. It would make me into a worthwhile person, it would give me the love I crave and I would give it the affection and love that my mother never gave me.

It is hard to be a parent at times, but in these dreams the dreamers feel betrayed, rejected, deserted and psychologically abused by the parents. Non-physical violence can be every bit as terrifying as physical torture, as in the rejection overtly presented in Jenny's dream:

> In a recurring dream, I am at home with my parents but they don't want me and I am trying to find somewhere to live.

Sarah's dream is also simple and direct:

> This morning I woke up dreaming my mother and her boyfriend were eating tons of ice-cream and wafers at my father's house. It was a lovely sunny day but they would not share their ice-cream. In real life neither of them works. My mother says she wants an easy life and certainly she's got one in some respects.

Meanwhile, even in her father's house, Sarah is not wanted. They will not share with her. She is excluded.

This longer dream, described by Flora, brings out a number of issues:

> This is the most vivid dream I can remember. I felt a terrible pain in my ears. I discovered that my mother had stuffed my ears with cotton wool and stuck something through my tongue. I was very angry about this. I went into hospital and discovered my parents were lying there in beds. My father was covered with a sheet, and he half threw it back to reveal a very hairy body. My mother was reading a book on shellfish. I told them I was discharging myself from hospital, and my father said bitterly: "I have waited all my life for you to come here and now you're leaving." By this time the pain in my ears had disappeared. I might add that my parents' marriage was not a happy one, and they are now, belatedly, divorced. I feel these dreams hold the key to my feelings about my family. But I wish they were more pleasant and not so disturbing.

There is an air of 'sickness' in this dream. Mother prevents daughter from hearing and talking; she prevents her from using normal means of communication, which angers Flora. There is the image of 'discharge': Flora is 'discharging herself' and some emotion needs to be discharged or released. She is signing herself out of this unhealthy place, and by the end of the dream the pain in her ears has disappeared. She manages to assert herself and, although she may wish that her dreams were less disturbing, they are putting her in touch with family relationships she has not yet come to terms with. There are certainly ambiguous messages in a number of Flora's dream images — for instance, in the father's gesture of invitation and revelation. The clever play on words — 'shellfish' sounds so like 'selfish' — aptly describes attitudes within the family.

As an adolescent, Mandy's antagonism found an outlet in dreams:

> I dream that I am out on my paper round, and come back to find my family have died in a fire and only the dog gets out. In another dream, I see my parents' home as a sheet of newspaper, burning, with me outside unable to do anything. Other dreams are about accidents and deaths in my family where I would be left on my own.

Fire destroys and purifies. In dreams it also provides an impersonal means of obliterating those who cross us. As I've said earlier, though, dreaming that a person is killed does not mean that you actually wish this to happen in waking life; rather, such dreams reveal that you may have hostile feelings that would be better dealt with than left festering and fermenting to erupt violently. Finally, Mandy is left in peace and quiet, and the dog, who never caused her bother, conveniently escapes death!

> For the last three months I've had the same type of dreams, which are so vivid I can remember all of them. The first one was more of a nightmare. Someone or thing was in bed with me hanging on to my back. I was shouting to my mother for help but no sound was coming out. I could not make her

> hear me, and my husband woke me up. I was threshing about and making terrible noises. Since that night I've been lost and attacked in my own town, still shouting for my mother. I've been late for a meeting trying to phone her, but all the phone boxes are out of order. I've been lost in a strange country and cannot make anyone understand I want a taxi to take me to the airport where my parents are waiting for me.

These recurring dreams began after Joyce's parents died. They show how much she longs to communicate with them but lacks the means to do so: the 'phone boxes' won't work. She is weighed down, symbolised by something 'hanging on her back', which she can feel but not see. In grief, much is invisible to us, though the raw emotion is devouring.

> And this way of nature is the way in which all things come into being out of darkness into light, then pass out of light back into darkness, the two principles — light and dark — being in perpetual interaction.
>
> *Joseph Campbell*, Myths to Live By, p118

BROTHERS AND SISTERS

We've all heard about, if not experienced, sibling rivalry, that terrible jealousy between offspring that can become almost murderous. Lauren's dream shows how injured she feels by her brother:

> I remember a dream where my brother was terrorising me with a snake. He was also throwing my mum's best crystal at me, which, when landing on me, shattered and buried itself into my skin. I was crying and ran to my bedroom. He followed me and opened the door slightly to show me the snake, then he dashed in and threw the snake round my neck. I screamed and woke myself up.

In Lauren's dream, we witness a fight for survival:

> I had this nightmare when I was a child. I am in a room with my brother, in a house where we used to live, and we are hiding behind a table. My uncle and other men are in the hall fighting with a monster, which is trying to come out of the cellar. I go into the hall, and the monster follows me into the room. I hide behind the sofa and the tiny monster goes to my brother, then aged about 4, and strangles him.

Nadia had a very disturbing dream about her cousin. It stuck with her, and although there were no outward problems, she decided to talk to her:

> When I told her about my dream she poured out all her problems, which she'd never mentioned before. I was shocked to find out what was going on.

At an unconscious level, Nadia recognised the unspoken emotional distress. Maybe it was a change in how her cousin dressed or her tone of voice. She picked up these non-verbal communications subliminally and her dream brought it to conscious awareness.

Grandparents

Grandparents play an important part in our lives, especially where they provide an escape from fraught relationships at home.

> I always used to dream about my parents being killed by my brother and I, so that we could live with our grandparents. But we always used to push our car, which wasn't our car, over a cliff. I always used to wake up with a wet face and hair from crying.

When grandparents die it is often the first time we have been bereaved, and our dreams reconnect us to the person who has died:

> Sometimes I dream about my grandma. I dream that she is still living and she is laughing and joking — just like my grandma — and I wake thinking that she is still alive. I lie there thinking, and then it suddenly comes to me that it is not true, she is dead. It upsets me quite a lot. Sometimes I dream about my grandma actually dying and wake up really sobbing. I suppose it is normal for me to dream about her because I was really close to her.

Valley was 14 when her grandmother died, but her dream visitation was a comfort:

> Shortly after my grandmother's death I dreamt she was standing next to my bed watching me sleep.

Of course, we shouldn't over-romanticise family relationships. For Vera there is not much love lost:

> I often dream about my mother. These go in phases. In the last series I was shouting at her, not very nicely. That finished with a dream of my grandmother. I was paralysed but summoned up every bit of strength to tell her to get lost. It was wonderful but terrifying.

Vera is moved by intense determination to a verbal attack. She succeeds and feels terrific!

Home truths

Dreams help us to see a different side to ourselves than the one we like to accept. For example, Sally told me:

> My dreams are little digs in the ribs that remind me of my

> inconsistencies, or ways I am being dishonest with myself.

Very often we have an idealised picture of ourselves that is draped in ignorance or denial, and 'home truth' dreams can be a real revelation.

Sally had a series of dreams in which people were ignoring her or being unpleasant and hostile. After she had been working on her dreams for a while she understood that it was she herself who was setting up the hostility. She projected her feelings on to other people and laid the blame for disharmony on them. Through her dream journal work she understood that her behaviour — sarcasm, hyper-sensitivity and so on — led to people feeling very uncomfortable when she was in one of her 'moods'. Now, she recognises that in order to maintain healthy friendships, she needs to curb the insensitive side of her nature and ensure she is kind rather than cruel.

The protective drive

Whom do you care for? Many women's dreams revolve around issues of caring for, protecting or in some way being responsible for other people. Judy described one of her protective dreams:

> I am married and have one child. One day there is a fire in my house and my child is stood at the top of the stairs. As I am just about to reach her the stairs collapse and I fall into the fire.

We fear that we cannot save our children, as Judy's dream shows. In our attempts to protect others we may put ourselves in jeopardy. Another woman has to save her husband:

> I tried to catch a large knife, to stop it falling and injuring my husband.

Arifa rescues her brother:

> I have violent dreams where my brother is attacked by a number of men. I arrive and shoot the prominent member of the gang at point-blank range. The dream is very specific: I'd do anything to kill the person who threatens my brother.

Arifa feels closer to her brother than to any other member of her family. She cannot confide in her parents, with whom she lives and he was her confidante. Her brother, now living in Germany, is no longer at home to support her and, after a particularly disturbing recent family row, she dreamt that he was there comforting her. In her dreams she can protect and save him.

Sometimes what we hear on the news or read in the papers influences our dreams, and we connect the events to our own lives as we sleep. Bee dreams of disasters and terrible accidents following tragic news about other people, but the injured parties become her husband or children. Many women are much better at fighting for other people — their children, lovers, parents — than they are for themselves. This fits in with our traditional role as carers of others.

Dreams that tell you it's all over

Relationships sometimes feel like they have too many knots, which are impossible to untangle yet we do manage. Jessie was certain that her long-term relationship was made to last. Everything seemed as it had been for the three years she and her partner had been together — there were no arguments, no indications of things cooling off. However, a dream caused her to reassess that certainty:

> I truly thought I was in love with my boyfriend, but in the dream I was walking around with another guy, Tad, near to where my grandmother lives. I know Tad socially to be very placid, easy-going and that he has a good sense of humour. In my dream we had a deep, meaningful relationship and we were really in love. Tad gave me advice about my boyfriend.

> I could feel a kind of love with him that I had never felt before.

What are we to make of this? Does it mean that Jessie really was in love with someone she knew only slightly? What Jessie felt when she woke up was that the dream was trying to tell her something. Its impact made her reconsider her relationship, which she decided to end.

For Diane it was the opposite:

> Many years ago when I was depressed and unhappy about our marriage, I dreamt that my husband had died. I had been trying to think how to escape my problems, perhaps by leaving him. My dream included the feeling of desolation at his loss, and helped in my decision to make the best of staying.

Diane's dream helped her to realise that this relationship was still important enough to invest more time and love, which meant that their marriage took on new dimensions.

Antonia found the intensity of her dream so powerful that she decided to pay more attention to her dream messages:

> I dreamed that my wedding ring slipped off my finger. I immediately woke up, and because the dream seemed so real I proceeded to look for it in the bed, then I noticed I was still wearing it. In fact, it wasn't loose enough to slip off. The whole thing shook me although I didn't know why. This was about two years ago, and I hadn't given it any more thought, until earlier this year when a relative who I told about this dream pointed out that it could have been a warning that my marriage would end. I started divorce proceedings at the beginning of this year. Two years ago this was the furthest thing from my mind.

A ring symbolises eternity. Where we lose a wedding ring it may indicate loss of faith in the marriage.

Over a period of two months Donna had a recurring dream about three times a week. She said:

> I dreamed me and my boyfriend were in a car crash, and he got killed. We had been together for just over two and a half years. Shortly after these dreams we split up.

All kinds of dreams bring us insight:

> It was a dream about wartime, and the man I was going out with at the time and I were about to be killed by being crushed under a tank. At the last minute, I decided to run away (he was injured and couldn't move) to save my life. It made me realise I was trapped in an oppressive relationship.

> When I was growing out of a two-year relationship with an older man (34 to my 21), I would wake at night choking and gasping for breath — I was dreaming that he was holding my head under water and I was drowning. This nightmare made me realise that I was right to be leaving the relationship.

A house may represent an actual house or symbolise a person or a relationship. In the following dream narrative, the shaking house in need of renovation refers to Jeannie's stale marriage and her need to explore her own inner world.

> I was in an old house with my husband, and we were looking to see if we could renovate it. I discovered that it had a cellar and wanted my husband to come and look at it. He said he would come soon but right then he didn't have the time, and he wouldn't lend me his torch so I could go alone. I waited for him for a long time, and he kept saying he was busy. Then he said it was time to go home and got into the car. I didn't go with him but went down into the cellar alone.

> At first I was very frightened because there was no light at all there, and I had to feel my way down the stairs in the dark. But as I went down the stairs it got lighter, and at the bottom of the stairs it was almost like being outside in daylight. The cellar was full of strange things, like an old-fashioned set of fire irons on a stand, but instead of the usual brush and shovel and tongs it had a knife, fork and spoon, and there were lots of toys there including a very beautiful wooden rocking horse.
>
> I stood at the bottom of the stairs, and suddenly the house started to move. It frightened me and I ran back up the stairs. When I got to the top I looked back, and it was still very light down there and seemed very nice and peaceful, but there was still some feeling of menace. I went outside to find my husband, and he was gone, but it didn't matter. I found I had the keys to the house so I went back inside.

She has found the keys, found a source of illumination and knows this is a journey she can undertake on her own should she choose to do so.

YOU'RE TEARING ME APART

> When I had this dream I knew it was time for me to leave the man I had lived with for many years. The worst and most memorable part was where we were arguing, and then suddenly he was standing with my daughter's injured body dangling from his hand. I knew instantly that her injuries were caused by us tearing her apart. It was sickening.

The dream was the final straw; there was no denying how far the relationship had deteriorated, and she left. In other dreams women see themselves being hacked to pieces with axes, being shot or shooting others, cutting, chopping and torturing. In the vast majority of dreams, though, women are the victims, not the perpetrators of violence. And the setting is usually within the family.

Conflict in families is common; what varies is the extent and intensity of the conflict and the way in which we deal with it. Meave's feelings of powerlessness were buried deep in the raw experiences of a brutal childhood. She told me of a dream she has had since childhood and drew me a simple picture:

> I dreamt I was in church. Dead bodies, without any clothes, were piled up on the window ledges. I was locked in the cold church and I couldn't get out. No matter how hard I tried, I couldn't get out. I woke up screaming.

The dream started when she was 12 just after she woke up next to her mother, whose bed she shared. She couldn't wake her mother, who was cold. Terrified, she ran for her father, who sent her into the kitchen and then sent the other children to join her. He never told her that her mother had died, and for years she was afraid to ask where her mother had gone. Finally, she dared to ask and he said: 'She's under the ground. Finished. Dead. Don't speak of her again.' Meave never did, but you can see how the dream expressed that isolating pain.

If in dreams you are attacked, cornered or literally torn apart, ask yourself what it refers to. In a group I had organised for wives of prisoners, one woman dreamt of being cornered by crocodiles in a modern block of flats. There appeared to be no way of escape at the time, and she woke up in a panic. The dream came some months before when her husband, addicted to heroin, had become a snarling, wild 'snapper'. He was unable to control his violent moods, and eventually his wife sought refuge with her friend in the block of flats in the dream. He followed her there, and she felt so 'cornered' about what was happening to both herself and the children that she refused to give him the alibi he demanded to escape a stealing offence for which he was to be tried. The dream puzzled and frightened her, but she said it really made sense now, considering all the strain she had been under.

Cassie had just moved into her own house, and with her new independence had come new dreams. In Cassie's dream there is a threat from her father but eventual protection from her mother. Here, the mother is a successful rescuer:

> I dreamt that someone's neck and shoulders were covered in scratches. In the dream I was lying in bed when my dad walked in. He switched on the light and went for my neck and shoulders with a razor blade. The only way I could stop him was to pull at his nose. My mother came in and pulled him away. When I woke up I felt it had not been a dream at all.

Linda used her dream to clarify her family dynamics:

> I used to have a real nasty one about being attacked by demons: a cat with a woman's voice, a dog with a man's. I would be rendered helpless by a hideous saw-like buzzing inside my head, and they would savage me, sometimes to death. I would wake up feeling freaked out and shaken. After a lot of thought, I realised that the cat and dog represented my parents. The last time I had the dream I fought back and escaped.

Divorce

Anxiety dreams often stem from earlier experiences, though this may not be obvious to the adult. Laura remembers the day when, at the age of three, her mother and father split up:

> I can see my dad fully but I can't see my mum's face. I remember my mum crying and her walking up the street. After that I went to live at my granddad's.

The separation left an indelible scar, since then she has always felt afraid, unprotected and undermined. She has other dreams in which she has no control over events that will hurt or destroy her. Waking acceptance of that pain has been hard for Laura, and she always tries to shrug it off. 'What's the point? No one really listens, and I don't want my mum to feel guilty.' Instead she carried her grief inside. 'I think we dream because in real life we can't express our feelings or what we think,' she said. 'That's how it is for me.'

Sal had many disturbing dreams, especially after her divorce:

> The bad dreams only started after my first husband left me. For a year and a half after the divorce, they became more and more frequent. Since my second marriage, and with a lot of help and support from my second husband, they are less frequent, though he still has to wake me from my sleep sometimes when I am really upset. I sometimes feel quite ill as I cannot get them out of my mind.

There are a number of recurring themes:

> Falling down an endless staircase; confrontations between myself and my ex-husband or my husband's ex-wife. Sometimes they both appear together, and always they are threatening me with violence, then they lock me in a small, dark room. Another recurring dream of drowning in a very black pool. I am spinning round trying to get free ... I have dreams in which my parents die or people that I am close to are being abused. To be honest, sometimes I am very worried about my dreams. They seem so real that they remain with me throughout the day.

Dreams bring what we deny or cannot face in waking life to our attention as we sleep. Let them in and they will show you new paths.

Where people change — shape-shifters

Like Venus who is trapped by 'shape-shifters', those gods who take on another form in order to trick her, present-day dreamers meet these beings in dreams. Faces change, genders change and flesh gives way to science fiction robots, as you can see in the next dreams:

> . . . nightmare in which I was going out with a man, we married and had a child, but the child died and I discovered the man was a robot, and so was everyone in the city I lived in.

> This man has come to tell me that my husband has got three years instead of six months for killing two dogs. But every time I went out of the room, when I came back his face had changed to someone else's.

> My nightmares are the usual horror story stuff about murderers and vampires, but the most disturbing was one in which I dreamed that about 90 per cent of people were actually dead although they appeared to be living, but they did not know this because the people who were really alive, who were all attractive, lucky, intelligent people, did not have the heart to tell them.

These dreams often indicate an ambivalent relationship with the person you are dreaming about. Where the change is from human to animal form, the characteristics of the animal may apply to the person. In dreams of shamans such dreams are particularly significant.

Rehearsal dreams

As we found earlier, some dreams have a prospective function: they prepare us, show us different ways of doing things or new skills.

> I often find myself capable in dreams of operating machinery etc. that I could not do in real life. Before I learned to drive I was always capable of driving in dreams. Another thing is that in real life I'm fairly short-sighted and wear glasses most of the time, in dreams I'm hardly ever wearing glasses and I can always see perfectly!

There may be a compensatory aspect to the last dream, but the others both inspire confidence and transfer into waking life.

> They give me space to rerun situations as many times as necessary until eventually the pain of the real situation to which they relate eases off. They sometimes rehearse the worst possible case and result in a reduction of fear towards the individual elements. They give a sense of wholeness to the messy experiences of everyday life by slotting them into some framework. Overcoming 'alienation' maybe.

We have looked at dreams of rape, but I include this one here because it relates to the way in which dreams can inspire confidence.

> There is one dream I remember that helped me realise I was stronger than I imagined. I lived alone for a long time and used to be nervous at times of intruders etc. This dream was where I was on a plane, I think, and there was a man who was about to rape me. Instead of being paralysed with fear as I would be normally, I stood up to him, and I either attacked him or walked away unscathed. I woke from this dream feeling tremendously powerful and excited about the fact that I had finally stood up to a fear of mine — that of attack and rape. I don't know that if the situation presented itself that I would act like that, but it greatly helped me psychologically at that time, and I can still remember it even though it is over ten years ago.

Venus at work

One aspect of writing or appearing on radio and television that I really enjoy is the contact with people who share their dreams. Often people write to me, as Isabel did. She heard me on the BBC programme 'Woman's Hour' and began recording her dreams. She told me:

> Since working with my dreams I've not so much changed as learned to accept and integrate parts of myself that I had long ago rejected. I feel I am a more rounded person.

Relationships at work get the dream investigation treatment too:

> Often dreams help me get rid of excess aggression — if someone at work, for instance, has annoyed me, dreaming that I am telling them exactly what I think of them is a good outlet. That's how my dreams are helpful to me. They are important to me in another sense. My work is, I suppose, fairly high-powered, decisions involving large amounts of money etc., and it's good to have an alternative, child-like, irrational side to the personality to balance things up.

Finding that balance in life is very important, as we will see in the next chapter. Where there is real danger, then a vivid dream will highlight the problem. When Valerie was at the end of her tether at work, she had this dream:

> I am falling over the edge of the banisters and only just manage to hold on.

The dream was the prompt Valerie needed to recognise the stress she was under — she was barely hanging on because she was under so much stress. She talked things over with a colleague and began to work positively on the conflicts that were pushing her 'over the edge'.

When your boss gets you down

Sometimes dreams let you know that relationships at work are just too much. This may be dramatically presented, for instance, by dreaming that you can't communicate because of the other person is speaking French, say, while you are speaking English, or the telephone won't work. If these dreams don't alert you then you might find yourself with a real attention-grabber, as Karen was, and she knew she had to act:

> I dreamt I killed my boss, and it made me realise I had to leave my job.

Venus and Mars at work may find clashes that do not improve the working environment. Wendy explained her situation:

> I work with a group of men and experience difficulties with their sexism. When this reaches a particular height I'll have dreams that encourage me to look at my inner resources and value my judgement and intuition. Recently after a distressing time at a conference, being the only woman in my tier of management, I had a dream where I was visiting a warehouse where you could exchange objects. I took in an old headboard and put it in a skip, and the man behind the counter offered me a number of old and dusty items in exchange. I knew I didn't want these and refused his offer.
>
> I was drawn to a pile of prettily embroidered children's clothes and then saw a pile of brocaded material. I lit up when I saw this and pulled out a length of green brocade and went away very happy, knowing I could use this in any way I wanted. I woke up feeling much better than I had in days, and knew that I could choose to work in a way I wanted to, that I could refuse the way of the men and make of my job what was appropriate to me.

She recognised that she could bring her feminine approach,

symbolised in the rich brocade, into her working practice and she could choose the 'children's clothes', the unrestricted, creative aspect of herself.

On her way to the top, Jill was anxious that she would 'get above herself', as her mother used to say. She had a recurring dream:

> I'm going up in a lift. It keeps going up and up, and I feel that the building seems endless in height. A great feeling of fear as the building seems to sway and an overwhelming fear of actually getting to the top and being so high up. Occasionally the fear I feel actually wakes me up.

Once she realised that it this was related to 'the glass ceiling' at work and that she was good enough to get to the top, then the dream disappeared.

Coming to terms with loss

Being lost may represent feeling lost on an emotional level, or in your career or may signify a feeling of lost spirituality. These dreams carry clues about where the problem lies and how to resolve it. Sonia had recurring dreams of her husband following his death. In one, there is the aching sense of loss — not dramatic, not spectacular, instead the routine, domestic meal-time scene that will never be repeated:

> *Dream 1*
>
> I could not understand why Rex was not there for the evening meal, even though a place was set for him. I kept slowing up the cooking and rewarming the plates and looking at my watch and wondering where on earth Rex could be.
>
> *Dream 2*
>
> I dreamed of Rex. I never actually saw him but I knew it was Rex. He was about to be married to someone the

following day, and I was doing my best to prevent it. He really preferred me, but he was still going through with the wedding.

Dream 3

Crying because Rex was dying. He was staying with Tony's dad. I wanted to go to him. Tony had been and said it was no use because he was in a coma and mumbling. I went — in an old, uncomfortable car. Much to my surprise, he was standing, mute and sad and looking very ill, by the side of Tony's dad outside the house. For some reason I couldn't stop directly outside the house, but pulled up some yards further on. I kept thinking that Rex would want to know why I was using an old car. Susan said I would have to buy new clothes for the funeral, and I said that it would have to be a very special outfit. Then I was driving down a backyard, and there were bin bags and boxes barring the exit. I got out of the car to go and move these, and one or two boys were collecting for charity and asked me to contribute. I shooed them away and said that I would give them a contribution after Rex had died, and that if he didn't die I would pay outright for whatever it was they wanted.

This dream series encompasses the raw emotions following the death of someone we love. There is disbelief, a refusal to accept he is gone — 'a place was set for him'. Sonia feels betrayed because he has gone, and this is symbolised in the part where 'he was about to marry someone else'. There is old, discarded stuff that must be dealt with, 'bin bags and boxes' that block her progress, and there is the bargaining we go through when someone is dying — she will pay the boys if Rex doesn't die. There are so many elements to this dream series, including the slow journey in the old, uncomfortable car, a psychological journey that Sonia did not want to make. The 'outfit', which must be fit to show someone 'out', at death, are all symbolic elements that mark the path of grieving.

Later there was another dream:

> Someone took over my body. Then there were two of us, and I commented that we looked remarkably alike.

In grief we often feel that someone has taken us over. Part of us goes on to automatic pilot and does the everyday things we have always done, while another part is travelling through the dark night of loss. Dreams can help us through this process. They do help us heal, as you will find in the next chapter, 'Healing Dreams'.

CHAPTER 5

HEALING DREAMS

The healing power of dreams comes in many ways: the healing of the body, the healing of inner wounds, and the healings of setbacks, losses and griefs.

Rosemary Ellen Guiley

Healing is the restoration of health and well-being. When life is out of balance, when we are physically overstretched or emotionally overwhelmed, what happens is that our immune system is compromised and then we are likely to become ill. What we can do is use our dreams to bring balance back. We can use them in a holistic way to get well and enrich our lives.

ANCIENT DREAM HEALING

Using dreams as part of the healing process has been around for thousands of years. The ancient Greeks built temples to the god of healing, Asclepius, where the sick would go, spend the night and receive a diagnosis or cure in their dreams. Hippocrates, the father of modern medicine, Aristotle, the great philosopher, and Galen, a famous Greek physician, all believed that dreams had a part in diagnosis and healing.

In ancient Mesopotamia, as in ancient Greece, there were temples devoted to the incubation of healing dreams. One, from about 3,200 years ago, recalls a woman named Mahituaskhit, who was unable to become pregnant by her husband, Satni, a high priest of Ptah. In desperation, she decided to sleep in the temple of Imhotep and had this dream, which started with a voice speaking to her:

> Aren't you Mahituaskhit, the wife of Satni, who are sleeping in the temple to receive a remedy for your sterility from the hands of the god? When tomorrow morning comes, go to the place where Satni your husband usually bathes, and you will find a colocasia (a water-plant) that is growing there. The colocasia root that you find you shall gather together with its leaves, you shall make a medicine from it that you shall give to your husband, then you shall lie by his side, and you will conceive by him during the same night.

Mahituaskhit followed his advice, became pregnant, and had her longed-for child. These Esclepian or curative dreams were eagerly sought and oracles grew up throughout ancient Greece and Rome.

Today, while we do not have such temples, the curative tradition continues. Cancer surgeon Bernie Siegel regularly incorporates dreams in his work with patients with life-threatening illness. He wrote in *Peace, Love and Healing*:

> Whenever people have to make decisions about their medical care (or anything else important in their lives, for that matter), I ask them to describe their illness, draw pictures of their situations and tell me their dreams.

The dreams turn to our own 'inner doctor' or 'archetypal healer' for information and direction, as we will see.

Sleep: the natural healer

> Dreams may be temporary flights into madness that, by some law of neurophysiology unclear to us, keep us from actual madness.
>
> *Joyce Carol Oates*

Anyone who has ever suffered from insomnia or had stretches

without sleep knows how much lack of sleep wears you down. Likewise, in periods of great change, where you have to adapt to totally new surroundings or, in extreme cases, after brain injury from chemicals or drugs, for example, following an attempted suicide, there is an increase of REM for a period far longer than the apparent time it took for the person to adapt or recover. As Sophie said:

> When my children were small less than four hours' sleep would mean daily life would start to be taken over by dreams after four nights. In fact, I did break down but made a full recovery. I think we dream to prevent mental illness, which in my humble opinion is dreaming while awake and trying to avoid rest.

As we saw in Chapter 2, dreams are essential for processing our daily experiences and weaving them into the whole fabric of thoughts, feelings and emotions that make us the unique human beings we are. Memories become consolidated as we dream. Robert Stickgold from the Harvard Medical School says in *Cycling in Your Sleep*: 'I used to say that sleep was just a preferred time for learning but now I'd say that certain parts of learning can't happen without sleep.' In fact, our bodies are speaking to us all the time, particularly when we sleep and the excess noisy interference of waking life is switched off.

Prodomic dreams

Prodomic is a word which comes from the Greek and means 'to run before'. Prodomic dreams, which have been recorded throughout history, are those which come before the onset of illness. They often begin in childhood. As a child, Joanna had a recurring dream featuring a witch and a castle. She realised it was a warning dream because invariably after it she caught childhood diseases such as chicken pox and measles. At a symbolic level she is 'captured' by something that is more powerful at that point in her life. On a practical level, once you know your warning prodomic dreams, you can look after yourself more carefully and prepare for and possibly avert the illness.

This one of Jane's is a typical migraineur's warning dream:

> One of the few black and white dreams I have had — I was a minute figure in a vast landscape — the vault of the sky was so high and the horizon so distant I seemed to be on the surface of a much larger planet than the earth. The tones of grey were as dull and flat as a newspaper photograph. I felt there was no point in looking about me — there was nothing near enough to be within the scope of my vision. Then there appeared a vivid red and blue scintillating, revolving disc in the grey sky, like a sun or planet. It was so dazzling that a pain shot through my eyes and head. I simultaneously opened my eyes and awoke in the darkness. To my horror, I could still see the flashing, whirling disc above and to the right of me. It took me some seconds to work out that this was the beginning of a migraine attack, with the usual visual disturbance. This is the only occasion when I have seen something in a dream that was still visible on waking.

Other dreamers have experienced dreams of terror and horror preceding a migraine attack. This is probably related to stress, physiological or emotional. The ability to handle emotional tension associated with stress provides one of the most successful ways of preventing migraine attacks. Dreams communicate inner conflicts that lead to stress, and by learning how to recognise these, the dreamer may then address the difficulties and so reduce stress. If you suffer from migraines you can use dreams as a predictor of the onset of an attack, as I explain in my book *Dreams, Counselling and Healing.*

Dominique, who lives outside Paris, had a terrible car accident. Doctors did not know if she would be able to walk again and thought for some time that they would have to amputate, at least her right leg, which was the most badly affected. Fortunately, they did not, but Dominique had to use a wheelchair. Her dreams changed after her injury:

> When I could not walk and was still in a wheelchair, I dreamt I was walking but more often I dreamt I was swimming.

For a long time her dreams had the same theme — walking, legs, feet, shoes, and so on. Now that she is starting to have a 'normal' life her dreams are more like the ones she used to have before her accident. She spoke of earlier dreams:

> I know dreams can be related to our future. Before my accident I dreamt of a great black lobster on my right leg, the one that has been injured the most.

For Dominique this was an early indication that there were unseen problems with her leg.

Healing people we love

Addiction causes problems in relationships, in work and in health. For the partner of an alcoholic, dreams tell the tale which we may ignore in waking life:

> Years after I left my husband because of his alcoholism I dreamt about taking a walk by the side of a stream. Lying in the stream, half-drowned, was a naked man (I did not recognise him as my ex-husband). I ran to him and half turned him over. I then thought to myself that I must cut out his liver in order to save his life. I think I started to do this but it's not clear. On reflection, I believe it was my unconscious mind telling me that if I had cut out his diseased liver I would have cured him of his alcoholism.

Celia has used her dreams for health and healing:

> I would say most dreams are healing if they show us our own mistaken perceptions of reality — once we understand our part in all our dramas and own illnesses, we are bound to heal them. Dreams also give us the opportunity to face our fears and confront them on an inner level and to bring issues from the subconscious to conscious mind. Once we accept something it is liberating; it is the fear itself that is frightening.

Prodomic dreams by proxy

Prodomic dreams do not need to be about our own health. There are times when we dream of other people's illnesses before there are overt symptoms, as Dervla did:

> My mother had two really bad illnesses when I was still at home. Before each illness I had a dream. Under her bedroom was our front lounge. In my dream I was trying to keep this big, black, evil thing away from her. I had got to keep it in that room and she would be okay, which I did. And she came through.

Clearly, Dervla knew intuitively, perhaps because of subtle changes she had noticed at a subliminal level, that her mother was about to be ill. This insight, unacknowledged during her waking life, forced itself into awareness in her dreams.

Depression

Gillian has recurring dreams of being smothered. She told me:

> I think my dreams of being smothered are symptomatic of the kind of life situation that has caused me to be depressed over many years. I feel my personality is being crushed.

This may have stemmed from the time she was sent away to boarding school and was desperately unhappy. In her dreams then she dreamt she was running and getting nowhere. Later she used to sleepwalk — all symbolic efforts to escape.

> I have recently felt less depressed, and I consider that two vivid dreams played a part in this. The first was one in which my dead mother came up to me in Charing Cross Road looking young, happy and slim, as she did in the photos I saw of her with my father. It was as if she was letting me go and allowing me to be happy. The second was a more vivid experience. My father died when I was six, and it took me a long time to realise how much I have lacked a father figure. Just before I started to feel less depressed, I had what I can only describe as a waking dream of my father in which I seemed to be wide awake but to be actually in his presence, or rather his presence seemed to be all around me. It was very comforting, loving and encouraging, and it was as if he were smiling at me, urging me to go on living and reassuring me that things were fundamentally all right and that he was part of me and had not in fact left me.

Depression is an illness that affects one in ten people. An early indicator that things are amiss is often found in dreams, as it was for Lily:

> As I go off to sleep a dreadful feeling of blackness comes over me. I try to stay awake but always fall asleep, then this thing so black and evil is standing by my bed. It's calling me to go with it, it has no form or shape, it's so evil and black. I always wake crying out, and on some occasions screaming and terrified. The dream leaves me upset for days after, and just when I think the dreams have left me they come again. For a while I linked them with the pain I have from my arthritis, but soon dismissed that. I am 40, I have a good husband and no real problems. These dreams have been

> going on for over a year now. I'm not a good sleeper at the best of times. I feel I am either being warned of something to come or punished for something I've done, and I'm worn out thinking as to what it can be.

The dream of the shapeless, evil, fearful thing that calls may symbolise the fear of the 'shapeless' unknown that lies ahead. No longer bound up only with the role of mother, Lily lacks direction and feels inadequate or unsure of herself. This is not unusual for women who have devoted their lives to raising children and being the homemaker, but now there is some decision to be made about the next phase of life. These decisions can be frightening — she can choose not to do anything but then may regret lost opportunities, or she could become paralysed, afraid in case it is a bad decision.

When we try to find out what our fears are, and do something about them, we discover that these disturbing dreams do change. Women who feel undermined, ignored and with poor self-esteem are much more likely to suffer from depression. Nightmares can help us face our deepest fears in a non-life-threatening way. In waking life some people who feel down go out of their way to dream about someone or something they like.

Rebecca, a student in her third year at university, has periods of depression that reflect difficult times in her waking life. In her dreams at these times, the colour is generally black and she feels trapped, just as she does when awake. The setting varies: a deserted city street, a dry desert or a house:

> I was locked in a house in which the interior was absolutely black. There were no windows, all light was excluded ... I woke to find I had leapt out of bed and was tearing at the walls with my nails. I could actually feel fibres weaving and growing together to trap me and close me in.

Her 'house' is as dark as the depths to which, in her despair, she sinks. There is no illumination, no light to pierce the dark, but she does find her dreams useful:

> I often feel that I am at war with them yet I know they are of value to me. I feel that whatever makes me dream is "sulking" because it considers that I misunderstand it. I suppose what I mean is that I am unaware of certain faculties or motives within myself, and this restricts my dreaming self.

It restricts her to the extent that she feels she should respond to the more positive messages that her dreams give, but takes no action. However, she wakes up feeling fresh, alive and vital when she recalls dreams, even if they were dull, because they help her, as she says, 'get in touch' with herself.

In the following description, you can chart the dreamer's progress from depression to confidence, a 'long' journey with lots of baggage. The loss of a leg, taken by her husband, disables Mary, but she does not give up, and she can still move.

> I was on my bike and trying to get ready to cycle somewhere, and I knew it was going to be a long journey because I had a lot of luggage piled on the bike. My husband was standing beside me and telling me I was too old for journeys like that. I had tried to ride away, but he grabbed my arm and I fell off the bike, and when I did one of my legs fell off and I sat on the road crying. My husband was shouting at me about how he told me so, and I kept trying to stand up but kept falling over because I only had one leg. I could balance if I held on to the bike but he kept trying to take the bike away, and then he stood there holding the bike out of my reach and I was crying.
>
> But there was a wall near me, and I found I could hop along if I held on to the wall, which was better than falling over, but I still kept crying because I wanted my leg back. I could see that I was coming to the end of the wall, but I could see there was another wall if I could just manage to

> hop across the street, and while I was crying to get myself together to let go of the first wall to hop across to the other one I woke up.

With support, symbolised by the wall she leans on, she carries on her way.

The events of trauma have to be remembered and integrated rather than attempts made to forget them. Garland's book *Understanding Trauma* warns of unresolved grief being passed down the generations of families. This is sometimes apparent in anxiety dreams or nightmares:

> I walked into the sea and quite painlessly drowned. My family and myself were powerless to do anything about it.

> Not long ago I dreamt I went outside — it was raining and I was depressed, but then I noticed blossom appearing on the branches of the bare trees. The other night I dreamt I went outside to be surrounded by colourful spring flowers.

As a person improves, and as their psychological health improves, the person takes a more active role in her dreams. She is less of a victim and can 'take off'.

> I remember a vivid dream where I was flying above a street of high-rise buildings, brightly coloured, though there was no-one in sight. I experienced feelings of joy and almost ecstasy, and felt totally uplifted.

Stress

> Charcoal under pressure becomes a diamond.

At times of stress anxiety dreams usually increase. Deborah sometimes has nightmares where she is in total darkness:

> Recently, I had a really stressful time. My husband has changed his job, which means a move. We have been kept in suspense about the details affecting our future, and this came out in an anxiety dream where I cried and poured my heart out to Boy George! I woke to find I had been crying in my sleep — which had never happened before. The dream was helpful as it certainly relieved tension — though goodness knows what Boy George thought!

Our mind has the power to influence us not only emotionally, but physically as well. In September 1998 Dr Jon Kabat-Zinn, of the University of Massachusetts, reported an experiment with a group of 37 patients with psoriasis. All of the patients were treated with ultra-violet light therapy, but half of them were also given relaxation tapes to listen to. The tapes focused on breathing and encouraged patients to visualise the ultra-violet light slowing down the growth and division of their skin cells. Those using the tapes found their skin conditions cleared 38 times faster than those who did not. 'This study demonstrates that the mind can influence an observable healing process,' says Kabat-Zinn, who established 'mindfulness meditation' in medical settings some twenty years ago. He has now influenced nearly 200 other medical centres to use this approach.

Stress shows up in our dreams, particularly if you are a mother who has a full-time job outside the home as well as in it:

> I have lots of anxiety dreams. Recently I was worrying a little about my son coming home from school in dreadful weather. He'd had a bad day, grazed his leg in the playground. I dreamt I had a young baby to care for, but I had to go out so I put it in a carrier bag because I couldn't find the carry cot. And as I rushed down the road I kept thinking I'd take it out and cuddle it before it got shaken up too much, but I still didn't get time. When I arrived home and tipped the bag on to the table out fell a scraggy chicken!

The 'scraggy chicken' symbolises how she feels after rushing around like a headless chicken most of the time! Except that her head is telling her that she needs to look after the baby, which may well represent herself.

Examinations

Some dreams indicate understandable anxiety about a forthcoming test, be it the traditional exam at school or another stressful situation such as an interview. For many of us there is an almost Pavlovian response: we hear the word 'examination' or 'test' and we immediately become anxious. Catherine, for example, had anxiety dreams before she sat her university finals. She had a recurring nightmare that her hand was chopped off.

Examinations in most cultures are a sort of rite of passage. If you pass successfully, then you are allowed to go on to the next stage, and in the really important ones you are given a special piece of paper that certifies that you have particular capabilities. Such endorsement provides a label that is frequently used to classify people. When someone passes a final exam, their status changes, perhaps from dependency to independence. Often, anxiety dreams about examinations highlight a feeling of immaturity and lack of confidence. Louise regularly has such dreams at anxious times:

> In the dream I am about to sit an exam and have forgotten everything I know.

Like Mona, she feels unprepared or lacks a vital piece of equipment:

> Finding myself back at school, I am unprepared for a lesson or an exam, or I'm in an exam but either I've got no pen or I've been given the wrong paper. Somehow I can't get anyone to help me.

This dream indicates the need to prepare for some testing event to minimise disquiet. If you have such a dream, try to identify a situation in which you are presently involved or are anticipating and which you see as a kind of test. Then consider what it is about the situation that is causing anxiety. Are you prepared for it? Are you lacking in confidence? Does it evoke that same feeling you had when you were a schoolgirl sitting exams on which your future depended? Are you afraid that you won't make the grade?

Quite often the dream examinations described to me are ones that the dreamer had successfully passed years before. Angela's dream offers reassurance:

> The clearest way I have of letting myself know that some situation is causing me anxiety is when I dream of doing exams. It is usually a Latin exam and I haven't studied an important work that is being examined. However, I somehow manage to get through it, just as I do in waking life.

Dreams offer a release from the pressures and stresses of day-to-day existence. They are our natural, in-built safety valve.

> Many other dreams I have are about diving and finding antique shops that always have beautiful things in them. I have recurring dreams about a house with many beautiful rooms, but they are often down dark corridors or up numerous steps, but I always get there in the end. These feel very healing. Over the past two years I have had significant dreams about black women as I have done work on coming to terms with and healing my racism.

Marie has had a number of stressful times in her life. However, now she has a recurring dream that usually comes when she is feeling peaceful and secure. She said:

> I am usually alone, wandering about in a house that is of a very unusual design. I get delight from wandering along corridors and up a staircase and finding nice rooms leading off. It is not an enormous house, however. As a child I had plenty of space to myself and together with a friend used to make up fantasies and use rooms in the house to enact them in. It seems that the 'fantasy' structure of the house has remained and returns to me at times when I am feeling most secure in my life.

In some cases stress becomes unbearable and may lead to 'breakdown', as Rosemary found:

> I dreamed I knocked someone down on a crossing night after night. Then, some months after this dream had recurred again and again, I was driving along a country road in Durham and just went to sleep. I woke up in a ditch with the fire, police and ambulance all trying to get me out of the car. I spent eight months in hospital with terrible injuries and a nervous breakdown. According to doctors, I was having the breakdown before the accident.

If someone is 'knocked down' again and again in your dreams, ask yourself if it part of you that is being struck down. Do you need to be more conscious of your physical and mental well-being? Remember, dreams come in the service of health and wholeness; they are concerned with your best interests.

CANCER

Illness is often a 'wake-up' call, a call to look at your life and what it means to you, to change self-destructive patterns and do what you are meant to do. Dr Bernie Siegel, cancer surgeon and author of *Love, Medicine and Miracles*, advised:

> Try not to die, that wastes your life; try to live. If you have

> cancer it's a blessing really, it allows you to prioritise. You have the right to choose how you live your life.

Numerous studies have shown how stress impairs our ability to produce natural killer cells, our white blood cells, which destroy cancer cells and help prevent virus infections. Chronic stress suppresses the immune system and leaves us more vulnerable to illness. The *Journal* went on to show that stress can even reverse the effects of chemotherapy, establishing credibility for techniques such as meditation to have a recognised role.

A speaker at the 1999 annual Cancer Self-Help Group's conference, where I ran a 'Dream Healing' workshop, spoke of a dream she had:

> A tall female physician said: 'You've got cancer.' I replied: 'No, I haven't.' I woke up scared and checked for lumps. Six weeks later I went to my doctor for a routine check-up. The short, male doctor looked at a bump on my nose. 'I have to cut a piece of your nose out,' he said after examining me. There was blood everywhere. 'I'm sorry,' he said, 'but I want to send it for a biopsy immediately because I think you may have cancer.' The waking experience was a reversal of my dream, but in a way it prepared me for his words.

The dream, as she said, prepared her and lessened the shock when cancer was diagnosed. Dreams in which a voice gives you information or advice can be important conduits for inner wisdom. Listen to them and reflect on what they offer you. Remember to think about the symbolism: 'cancer', for example, may be a metaphor for something that is 'eating away at you', a problem within the family, perhaps.

At another workshop at Warwick University, Bernie Siegel spoke of the importance of patients' dreams. A woman with cancer came to him. She was not sure whether she should go ahead with an operation that another doctor had recommended, and so she had come to Bernie for a second opinion. After the meeting, she was still undecided whether to go ahead or to avoid any kind of further medical intervention. They left the decision until the following week. The next time she came to his office she said she had decided against any treatment because she'd had a dream in which a cat had appeared, and the cat was called Miracle. In the dream she felt that she was completely cured and that she didn't need further treatment. This in fact proved to be the case.

In *A Coward's Chronicle*, the singer and actress Marti Caine described her experience of cancer, which changed her life:

> Since becoming aware of my mortality, the world has changed to technicolour and I'm in awe at the wonder of it all ... I'm surrounded by survival, despite the odds, and my own determination is renewed.

Threat

Catherine dreams vividly. This is one she had about six years ago:

> I have had a recurring nightmare for the last six to seven years. The dream quite simply is that someone is trying to murder me. It occurs in differing forms — different countries, different people involved, set in dark rooms, caves or open spaces etc. The strange thing is that I usually 'know' who the murderer is, witness him/her committing several murders on other people beforehand, and in so doing become a prime suspect in other people's eyes for these crimes. Just before I am to be stabbed/shot/whatever, I wake up.

What happened six years ago that could have triggered this dream? Was there an event Catherine remembered that she has still not come to terms with? The dream is certainly about fear. This dream may reflect something about Catherine that she is either suppressing or refusing to allow to consciousness, which is 'in the dark'. This could be anything, from displaying her true feelings in order to 'keep the peace', to not wearing the sort of clothes she wants to wear. She may be trying to destroy a part of herself which she, or someone else, disapproves of. In the end it is more helpful to recognise a part which we are not happy with than to pretend it doesn't exist.

Only Catherine will know if this could fit, but if you have a similar dream, try to honestly analyse the dream in terms of what parts of yourself could be depicted in it. Can you think of any things which you feel guilty about? In the dream people are accusing her, so are these real people or one part of herself accusing another part?

Ruby, a 19-year-old student, was having a difficult time living at home with her family. She told me:

> About four to six months ago I had a dream that strongly affected me: I often dream that I am in a house with my family (usually a bungalow and usually one we have lived in), and I am bolting all the doors and windows because there are wolves outside. But I can't make the rest of my family see this, and they open the windows and doors.

Animals in dreams are highly symbolic. What do you associate with wolves? Are they wolves who follow women or wolf whistles? Ruby seems to be under attack and is trying to keep them out of her house. She sees the danger but her family doesn't, can't or won't see the danger. This sense of threat is disturbing and a warning to Ruby that she needs to recognise that she feels unprotected. This may be because of her more independent role as a student, which is causing friction at home. Whatever the trigger for the dream, it would be helpful to discover what these wolves symbolise. She has interpreted this as meaning that her family don't understand her and she can't make them understand. She could imagine 'interviewing' the wolves to find out what they want and ask why they want to get in.

Mina recognises the importance of sleep and dreaming. She explained:

I think my health, particularly my mental or emotional health, suffers when I don't dream. A stark example is what happened to me after the birth of my daughter. I had an emergency Caesarean section in the early hours of the morning, and during the following days in hospital I found it very difficult to sleep. I became extremely distressed and confused and began having hallucinations. I became paranoid and believed that my mother wanted to take my daughter from me.

Looking back, I feel that, deprived of my dreams, I started living my nightmares. My sleep and dream time is when I feel I 'process' what is happening and try to make sense of things. Without sleep, nothing makes sense any more. There have been other similar episodes in my life, when I've missed too much sleep for one reason or another, and have started becoming confused and unable to concentrate. A good, long night's sleep when I can dream again has always got me back on track once more.

Breaking the habit

As we have seen, dreams highlight our anxieties and help to reinforce decisions we have made. They help with pledges we have taken, such as giving up smoking:

> I often dream that I am in the middle of a cigarette and am horrified when I remember that I have given it up. This dream is becoming less frequent as time goes on. I used to dream that I was driving, pursued by the police. This was when I had been banned from driving. I never had it when I got my licence back.

Sometimes the dream strengthens resolve by pointing out dangers:

> Before I gave up smoking, and for some time afterwards, I

> frequently used to dream that I had gone to sleep and left a lighted cigarette on the bed. I used to wake up groping about trying to find it.

HEALING OURSELVES

> According to energy medicine, we are all living history books. Our bodies contain our histories — every chapter, line and verse of every event and relationship in our lives.
>
> (p. 40) *Myss*

One of the most important parts of being alive is to discover who we are and what our life's journey is all about. Maslow calls this 'self-actualisation', and it means that while we do all the other things we need to in order to survive, such as find a place to live, have food to eat and play our part in the community in which we live, we desire more than mere survival. There is still a central core that needs to grow and reach its potential. This can be anything from painting to growing roses. Each one of us has to listen to the inner voice, which will guide us to soul-satisfying experiences, but often we are too frenetic to take the time, or we may actively avoid anything that involves self-reflection.

We can be our own worst enemies; for the sake of physical, emotional and spiritual health, we need to be our own best friend. Dreams can help us reveal all aspects of our nature.

> Recently I've dreamed of an affair with a male friend — a recurring dream. I'm only just realising he is another aspect of myself: he is always the nice guy, never gets angry, or down, never really shows much emotion, just agreeable, always ready to please. This is the 'front' I put on while silently seething inside at all the injustice around me. Now I'm ready to put myself first and do what I want to do — not what I 'should do'.

Paula Reeves, an inspired therapist and creative artist, explained that we need to listen to the messages of our dreams and bodies. As she said in *Women's Intuition*: 'When you do not know what matters to you then that becomes the matter with you.' We need to find out what is important in our lives, what 'matters' to us, if we are to maintain health in mind and body.

> Another recurrent dream is the most wonderful, graphic and soothing of all my dreams. Even remembering these dreams induces almost mystic, pleasant feelings. I find myself in paradise, Utopia or wherever. There are usually unbelievably scenic surroundings, mountains, trees, pleasing slopes or buildings — I always have panoramic view of these things — but most of all there is always a silky, warm stream or river for me to swim or glide along in effortlessly. Everything is perfect and effortless.

Healing dreams come in all forms. Whether the source of comfort is vague or defined, it restores and comforts us. Belief in the possibility of healing is important and it aids recovery, just as positive thinking has been found to build up the immune system, as described earlier. At its simplest level it may be simply to believe in the power of good, as symbolised in the final dream in this chapter:

> I had this dream when I was about five. I dreamed an angel appeared in the room and my mother explained about my illness. She gave me a blessing and I was instantly cured. In reality, I was a lot better the next day.

We can experience healing dreams at any age and at any point. All you have to do is open yourself to receive them. In the next chapter we will explore how the cycle of our lives is mirrored in our dreams.

Chapter 6

Life Cycles

Our dreams chart the physical changes we experience as women. Menstruation, ovulation, pregnancy and the menopause affect our dreaming lives and reveal emotional undercurrents that may go unnoticed during waking hours.

Meanings in the menstrual cycle

Dreams are affected by the menstrual cycle, as you may have already discovered if you have been recording your dreams. Therese Benedek, a psychologist, who researched the subject of menstruation and pregnancy, suggested as early as 1939 that the sexual content of women's dreams is influenced by the hormonal changes in the menstrual cycle. She explained that the psyche and the body are indivisible and that menstrual phases are accompanied by predictable changes in mood, including increased sexual desire.

Violent periods – pre-menstrual dreams

Pre-menstrual tension is worse for women who are deprived of rapid eye movement (REM) sleep, that is, dream sleep. Ernest Hartmann, in *The Biology of Dreaming*, suggests that changes in the menstrual cycle indicate a need for more REM sleep late in the cycle before menstruation. In fact, he points out the similarity between pre-menstrual tension and dream deprivation. This fits in with the findings of Serois-Berliss and de Koninck, who suggested in 1982 a correspondence between a significant increase in menstrual stress and an increase in dream anxiety and hostility.

Just prior to menstruation, many women have violent or bloody dreams. Linda, for instance, dreams about blood flowing:

> Last night I dreamt I was walking around the town. My chest wall was exposed as if I had been blasted. There were no ribs, just a gaping hole. I could see my heart and lungs and the skin flaps. It was all very bloody, but there was no pain at all. I was trying to cover it up with bits of gauze and thought I'd go to my mum's. She would suture it for me.

Linda was due to start her period the next day, and for her it was a typical pre-menstrual dream. Although the blood flows, there is no pain, which reflects the waking experience because Linda does not have period pains. The dream shows her chest bared, exposed and blasted. What might she need to get off her chest?

Jenny and Clare both suffer from pre-menstrual tension, and their inner turbulence is echoed in their dreams. Clare finds herself wielding sharp knives or other weapons, whereas Jenny has vivid dreams involving bloodshed and stabbings.

> Just before a period, I always dream about blood flowing from a cut. Either the next day or two days later I start my period.

Just before the onset of a period, as our bodies prepare to expel the lining of the womb, some women feel pain, cramps or lethargy and feel irritable. At this pre-menstrual stage these symptoms may cause feelings of aggression that show up in dreams. For Jenny and Clare, we see this in the stabbing pain that knives can inflict.

Penelope Shuttle, poet and author, was plagued with severe pre-menstrual depression and physical pain that medical treatment did not help. After years of searching she found that she had the answer herself: through dream analysis linked to her menstrual cycle, she was able to conquer the disabling aspects of menstruation and turn them to positive, creative attributes. She writes of this in *The Wise Wound*, co-authored with her partner Peter Redgrove, and it remains one of the most insightful books available on menstruation, myths and realities.

Menstruation

In *Creative Dreaming*, Patricia Garfield noted distinct changes in dreams according to where she was in her menstrual cycle, but she found that dreams during the menses were difficult to recall. In his research, noted dream researcher Robert Van der Castle found that during the menstrual period women had a more active role towards males in their dreams, as Diane confirmed. She finds that her menstrual dreams involve seeking out men to seduce. The most erotic dreams occur while she is having her period. She thinks this is because she is not worried about contraception at that point in her cycle and welcomes the freedom that menstruation brings.

Changes in the levels of oestrogen and progesterone in the body influence dreams and can guide each of us to discover our own sexual pattern and highlight times when sexual desire is at its height. Havelock Ellis noted this double peak as the 'menstrual wave of sexual desire', one during or around menstruation, and the second in the middle of the cycle. This pattern shows up in Tina's dreams, which are more vivid just before ovulation and during her period. Mainly, the dreams at both stages emphasise erotic sexuality. Tina says:

> I feel distinctly more sexy just after 'ovulation', in the middle of the month, and especially during my period. I experience sexual dreams around this time.

Many women are still influenced by taboos about menstruation. It was not so very long ago that menstruating milkmaids were banned from the milking parlour in case they turned the milk sour! Many cultures still insist that menstruating women keep themselves apart from the rest of the tribe. Looking further back in history, Pliny (*circa* AD 23–79) damned menstruating women. In his famous *Natural History*, he wrote:

> On the approach of a woman in this state new wine will

> become sour, seeds which are touched by her become sterile, grass withers away, garden plants are parched up and the fruit will fall from the tree beneath which she sits.

Men could not understand how women could bleed and not die. The menstrual taboo shames women and persuades some of us to take on board a negative self-image.

Ovulation

After recording her dreams for many years, Kate has identified a definite pattern. She finds dreams at ovulation involve holding or looking at small, delicate objects, especially jewellery. For her, 'small, delicate objects' are symbols of eggs released at ovulation, their gem-like fragility echoing the nature of the human egg on its journey from fallopian tube to uterus. A typical 'ovulation' dream from Kate's dream diary is rich with symbolism:

> I dreamt of cut-glass jewels, tiny, multicoloured cubes in my hand. One had a hole down the middle like a bead but it had broken in half so that there was a little furrow where the hole had been ... I took off some green alabaster scarab earrings only to find that one of them had cracked into four pieces though it remained in the setting.

Fertilised eggs divide first into two, then into four, and so on. It is as if Kate's dream continues that natural development in symbolic form. The voyage the egg takes in the hidden channels of her body is symbolically enacted:

> This dream was all about journeys. I had been on several different trains and then spent a lot of time walking down tunnels and across rough land ... I came to this rough track with a farm worker's cottage at the end of it where a man and a woman were standing. The woman was pregnant again, but she knew that this time she was going to give

> birth to a fish. As we watched, she delivered the long, smooth, greeny fish, which later changed into one of those sea-green ornamental dolphins. It was covered with big bobbly scales and had a curly tail and big lips. It was beautiful, translucent and glasslike ... Some time later I noticed in passing that the whole thing had fallen to the floor and smashed into tiny glass fragments. It did not seem important, though.

The final part of the dream indicates the disintegration of the unfertilised egg. Kate takes little notice of that since it is part of the natural order. She is in tune with her body and its rhythms. Like Kate, with methodical recording of dreams, you can develop a highly sensitive degree of self-knowledge, which reflects this union of psyche and body.

Benedek also found that dreams of precious gems, round fragile objects and delicate items were common during ovulation, as in this one which June had the day after she ovulated:

> I am going on a trip with my parents. We come to a youth hostel/hotel of some kind and when I go into my room there are bunk beds. There is a 12-year-old boy in the bottom bunk. He has been left behind while his party have gone off ... I also find a purse rather like a small make-up bag I have, and in it I find some semi-precious stones and a goldfish swimming around, although there is virtually no water in it. I want to get some more water for the fish as he seems lucky to have survived so far and should be all right if I act quickly.

June would like to have another child, and so she can if she acts quickly and takes care of 'the little fish'.

Fish in dreams are frequently linked to conception and pregnancy. Maybe it's a return to the embryonic sea from which we all evolved, the sea Venus rises from in her scallop. The 12-year-old boy represents June's son. He had been complaining that unless she got a move on, he would be 13 before he had a baby brother. Nothing in the dream is wasted. We find the characteristic journeying typical of this stage of menstrual dreaming, the semi-precious stones symbolising the egg and the fish. Just a hint of warning, though, that the life-giving water might be running low. June's son, the result of a previous conception, will be 'left behind', just as the boy in the dream has been 'left behind'. He is very firmly part of this picture, just as he is in waking life. He plays a central role in his mother's life, and his inclusion gives clarity to the dream narrative.

Such a dream is very useful. It tells June that she needs to get herself completely fit for childbearing if that is what she wants, and she has some serious thinking to do about whether or not to have another child.

Conception dreams

One of the characteristics of dreams right from the start of pregnancy is that they are so luminous. For some women, crisp, clear dreams of fertility are the first intimation that conception has taken place, occurring before indicators such as morning sickness, tender breasts or missed period. The quality of these dreams is recognisably different from other dreams. Women who have had 'conception' dreams had no doubts about their meaning. In *The Analysis of Dreams*, Medard Boss describes such an experience:

> ... the young woman who saw her body as a field through which a plough was cutting a furrow had, a few days previously and for the first time, unreservedly surrendered to the love of a man. She experienced this event itself as a 'natural event'. She had become pregnant without being aware of it at the time of the dream. These two events had so intensely attuned her whole existence that it seemed to overflow her human body and corresponded to Mother Earth herself, to a field ripe for sowing.

While Paula's situation lacked such subservient trappings, she too had a significant dream before she knew that she was pregnant. Working hard as a deputy head teacher of an inner-city comprehensive school in Leeds, she nevertheless found time to consider the dreams, particularly this one. It signalled the beginning of a pregnancy that was very difficult.

> I had a really exhausting dream. I was sitting in a room, and by the power of my thought I was moving this strange object through the air. It was like a clear plastic bag, the sort you buy pre-packed with olives in, only it contained a beautiful stone egg. I knew in the dream that I had to concentrate completely and utterly if this 'bag' was to get to the other side safely. I did it but it was incredibly hard.

Later Paula realised that she had been about 12 days pregnant when she had the dream, and 'knew' it was about having a baby. She did have a problematic pregnancy in which a threatened miscarriage and high blood pressure forced her to give up work and spend a large part of each day in bed. She had a son just before the expected date of confinement, but often felt it was sheer willpower that had kept her much-wanted baby going, just as her dream had indicated. She also had this dream:

> I could see a caterpillar in the freezer. I don't know how I knew it was a caterpillar because it didn't look like one. It was very thin and pale green and see-through. I took it out of the freezer and put it in the oven and it went fat and fluffy and started moving about. I can't explain that, can you?

The freezer is a place of storage. The caterpillar she took out was thin and pale green and see-through, rather like a spermatozoon, except for the colour. The caterpillar is a butterfly in the making. She takes out of her freezer and puts into the oven, a euphemism for womb in English. 'She's got a bun in the oven' is a colloquial expression to describe a woman who is pregnant. Then it comes out fat and fluffy and moving about. The symbolic birth process is complete.

Sexual desire

Carol has been involved with Jeff for five years and describes their relationship as steady and secure, yet she is flooded by disturbing dreams of sex, particularly during her period. Initially she is making love with Jeff, but then the lens takes in a wider scene:

> Suddenly a gang of bikers, big scruffy, hard men, burst into the house, wrecking everything, then they take me and my sister to rape. The gang ritual usually involves some ultimate in violence, some form of atrocity, but I always find that my rapist, the leader, comes to really like me. He is gentle and kind and doesn't go through with the task but escapes with me.

Though she feels stronger when she comes through unscathed in this and other dreams, Carol is still troubled by them. They continue the myth that 'romantic', handsome rapists can be changed by a 'good' woman. Her more subtle, 'Freudian phallic' dreams, as she describes them, which also appear during this stage of her cycle, are more disquieting and not nearly so romantically adventurous or sexually titillating:

> I dream of poisonous worms and snakes turning into men, chasing me and finally "spitting" venom either in my mouth or on my skin. It's deadly.

Carol is surprised at these dreams because she enjoys sex and has no inhibitions, yet there the dreams indicate some dislikes and fears; I wonder how she feels about oral sex? I stress *how she feels*, not what she thinks; there can be a tyranny in what is taboo in sexual practices as well as everything else. Such pressure prevents many expressing preferences, so it is important to concentrate on feelings rather than rationalisations. Does she feel that semen is 'venom', as in her dream? She has no desire to have children – in fact, she told me: 'I thoroughly dislike them. I harbour no maternal feelings at all.' Maybe that is why the 'venom' is so deadly to her.

The lunar cycle

The lunar cycle influences the reproductive cycles of all living creatures. The incidence of violent crimes, whether committed by men or women, fluctuates in accordance with the lunar cycle, and the term 'lunatic' reflects the link between mood and the moon. While our rushed lifestyles give us little chance to tune into the subtle variations of mood that may be affected by the moon, these influences do show up in dreams.

Dreams have been 'the light at the end of the tunnel' for Olive at times when the going has been really rough, and in her faithful work on dreams she has learnt many things:

> I have a very active dream life just before menstruation, and this is further reinforced when there is a full moon. Recently the eclipse of the new moon seemed to initiate a lot of powerful dreams, including a regression dream which took me back to an incident when I was 12 months old. The situation had been extremely painful, resulting in a lot of blocked anger and hurt. I am still working through this.'

Olive knows from past experience that such dreams help her to change negatives into positives, so she is empowered by her dreams. She told me:

> I've not so much changed as learnt to accept and integrate parts of myself that I had long ago rejected. I feel a more rounded person, on an exciting journey, a thrilling adventure, finding out about me. There have been bad times but, having said that, dreams represent the possibility for

> acceptance and change and greater self-awareness. They help us get in touch with our own humanity and our own spirituality.

Few women are as fully aware of the effects of the moon on their cycle as Olive. However, Tom Robbins, in his book *Still Life with Woodpecker*, drew a heroine, trapped and existing without any artificial light, living in total unison with the cycle of the moon:

> By May she was menstruating regularly at the new moon, just as the ancients did, and in July she observed that she had begun to ovulate when the moon was full, as will any healthy woman whose nights are not polluted by synthetic lighting. She could always tell when she was about to ovulate because her vaginal mucus would become wetter. Her glands were greasing the tracks, as it were, for the Sperm Express ... she had begun, inadvertently but successfully, to practise lunaception.

You can see how women's cycles are moon cycles. Maybe, like Julie, you'll find that your dreams are 'disturbing and restless when there is a full moon'.

Seasonal changes may also influence your dreams.

> I think for some reason that my dreams are more vivid and sweeter in the summer than in winter; less worrying. Maybe because, for me, there is only one season worth having. I'm always happier in summer.

Dreams as preparation for childbirth

Dreams are valuable in preparation for childbirth. Dreaming is found to help in shorter delivery times and fewer complications, as American dream researcher Patricia Garfield has noted. Pregnancy and childbirth are probably the most exciting and yet the most traumatic experience a woman can go through, voluntarily. We are all subjected to various traumas and injuries where we had no control over the events and their consequences, but a mother-to-be has nine months to prepare for the final labour and birth. No amount of ante-natal advice and care can prepare one for the actual process of childbirth.

Since dreams are known to be part of the process of learning and remembering, of problem analysis and 'data processing', it is logical to expect increased dream activity in women during the time they are pregnant. Some pregnant women start by having more frequent and more vivid dreams during the time they are expecting. Many dreams are to do with having the baby, seeing one's child and visualising it. These dreams can help the woman face fears and mental blocks regarding the baby, such as preference for a boy or girl and its well-being, and make her more capable of accepting the responsibility for her own feelings so that she is aware of what is going on inside for her.

MISCARRIAGE/ABORTION

Losing an unborn child, a miscarriage or spontaneous abortion, as it is called, can be a devastating experience. It leaves a residue of grief and fear that any future pregnancies will also be jeopardised. In this comprehensive dream record sent to me by Masha, we find the whole gamut of emotions:

> In spring 1991 I got pregnant. I was looking forward to having a baby. When I was pregnant nine weeks, I had this dream: there was a herd of cattle on a meadow and a bull among them. It was bleeding, its belly being torn and its intestines hanging out. I don't remember if there had been a fight with another bull or a man. The message seemed to be one of violence (but not directed towards me) and loss. When I woke up I was worried. Soon I started bleeding. In the 12th week I had a miscarriage. The doctor told me the embryo died when nine weeks old. Its death was, I guess, quite simultaneous with the dreams.

In November 1994 I got pregnant again. I was pretty scared in case of another miscarriage. And I dreamt of a big black bull again, but this time he was perfectly healthy and strong. Even dangerous. He was circling around the house I hid in. I didn't dare to come out, I was afraid he would hurt me. When I woke up I thought this was a threat. Again I began bleeding — in reality, not in my dreams. Little by little, nothing serious, only 'to scare me', from the first month on. My doctor said the baby was doing just fine, but I was still anxious. Weeks passed. I began to read your book *Women Dreaming*.

On March 20 1995 (in fourth month of pregnancy), I remember to have read Patricia Gerhardstein's dreams (p78) of a cup, firmly attached to a tree, representing healthy pregnancy. The story touched me deeply. I wished I had a similar dream to be sure everything was going to be OK. Then I fell asleep and had this dream: I am walking with a relative of mine who lives in the country. It is harvest time, beautiful colours, sun is shining, feeling of an overwhelming abundancy. We come to a kind of barn, *kozolec* (typical of Slovenia), but an unusually high one. There is a single grape attached to it, ripe, of a dark indigo colour, very beautiful and big, and placed unusually high.

I look up and say: 'You didn't pick this one?' 'No,' she says and adds firmly, 'we'll leave it up until autumn so that it ripens up.' You can imagine I cried a bit, I was so relieved and happy. On August 9 1995 I delivered a perfectly healthy baby girl. In this moment of writing I realised it was also partly because of this dream that her father and I chose the name Visnja for her (pronounced Vishnya), meaning not only 'of/from the sky' but also a sour cherry, marasca.

Masha's dreams show how powerful and healing our dreams can be.

Philippa saw this terrifying dream as a warning:

> I dreamed that a midget was chasing me with the intention of stabbing me in the abdomen with a stiletto knife. He said that, though I kept claiming to be pregnant, I couldn't be as I was too thin ... I awoke screaming and started to miscarry within 48 hours. I was 18 weeks pregnant at the time ... I really felt the dream foretold the miscarriage. Looking back, I was under considerable strain at the time, being four months pregnant and my first child only six months old. I didn't want the child subconsciously, and I felt the dream was about that. The pregnancy was not planned, and I was living in a one-room apartment with no bathroom.

Underlying fears surface dramatically. Philippa was 'too thin' and under attack from a viciously armed 'midget' who insisted she was not pregnant. She was too weak to fight off even the 'midget', and the dream threat becomes waking reality. The imagery is direct and needs little interpretation. However, unlike one researcher, who saw anxious dreams as being a major factor in 'foetal wastage', I would say Philippa's waking situation and physical condition played the major part, and her dreams revealed the extent of the threat.

Last year, Sally was devastated to discover she was pregnant. She and Kyle, her boyfriend of two years' standing, had talked about having children, in the way that couples do in a relationship that has long-term possibilities. Kyle was absolutely certain that he did not want to be a father. Sally agreed. She was 26 and wanted to continue her career and, though she did not feel as strongly as Kyle, she really was not bothered either way. But she did want Kyle, and she knew he would leave her if she had a child. The night she should have had her period, she had this dream:

> I dreamt of a man with a knife. I was terribly afraid. There was a big, thick towel covered in blood. It was my blood. I later discovered I was pregnant and had an abortion ten weeks later.

Sally's dream preceded her experience of a termination, yet it tapped into bodily awareness of conception and subsequent events.

This example, which was sent to the *Sundance Community Dream Journal*, edited by Henry Reed, an American publication devoted to dreams and dreamers, shows how reassuring some dreams can be. It is the one Masha refers to in her dream report earlier. Patricia Gerhardstein of Ohio had previously had a miscarriage and was very afraid that a miscarriage might happen again. She talked with her doctor, who suggested lots of bed rest. She wrote:

> I was in my third month of pregnancy and began to have some bleeding. I went to sleep and had this dream: I see a large, large, strong tree, with noticeable trunk and roots. Coming off the tree has grown a branch into a nearby wall. The tree and the wall are inseparable. From the attached branch a white cup hangs by its handle in such a way that there is no possibility for the cup to come off — it is permanently attached to the tree. The scene was filled with white light. I awoke feeling peaceful and happy, knowing that I would not have a miscarriage. At the end of the nine-month pregnancy I delivered a healthy baby girl.

An estimated one-third of all women will experience a miscarriage during their lives, and where life has been expected, the loss can be devastating. During the nine months of growth and preparation, most mothers-to-be consider the possibility of having a deformed or damaged baby. I certainly did, and I discovered later that I was not alone, yet too often it is considered neurotic or irrational to voice those fears. They are voiced, though, in dreams, as Sharon found:

> When I was pregnant I dreamt of giving birth to a headless, armless, legless monster. It was so vivid that I phoned my sister to tell her about it. Every time I'm pregnant I fear

> delivering a child who is less than perfectly formed — surely every woman does?

Abigail had a distressing dream while carrying her third child:

> I was in a room with people I knew and liked. I was happy to introduce my new baby there. As my sister lifted the baby from the cot — a slow-motion action — it became apparent to everyone, and especially to me, that my baby was grotesquely deformed. I noticed that he had an enormous, swollen, caved-in head, like a punctured football, floppy and hanging about. Everyone looked sorry for me but I felt only slight disappointment and still loved the baby. I then recall cuddling and comforting the baby.

She too had a healthy baby boy. In Abigail's case, her dream tells her that she has the love and warmth to sustain a good relationship with her 'grotesquely deformed' dream baby. It is no accident that in the dream room she is surrounded by people she knows and likes, indicating that there is unconditional support for her.

Drugs and illness in pregnancy

During pregnancy women are sometimes prescribed drugs that may cause anxiety. Annie was prescribed antibiotics for a slight urine infection. 'Then', she said:

> I had a dream that the doctor (female) had prescribed the wrong tablets for me, and advised me that this mistake could have affected the child and it may be born with some deformity but they would not know until after the actual birth. I am very wary of taking any drugs or medicine while pregnant in case the baby is affected, and this dream is, I think, a result of that wariness.

No wonder the first question after giving birth is usually 'Is the baby all right?' This apprehensiveness may be based on the knowledge that real dangers have been experienced during pregnancy, as in Sheena's dream described below, or may be a foggy fear which comes and goes and which has no identifiable source.

> I go into a grim hospital in a side street. My baby has been born but I have not been allowed to see it. I am a schoolgirl again, wearing my old school uniform ... Inside the hospital I meet a nurse, her arms piled high with babies like plastic dolls. I ask about my baby and am told it has all the handicaps feared for it, and worse. I ask what sex it is and am told it is too badly deformed to tell. I feel great guilt and despair.

The symbolism in this dream is highly revealing. The setting in a dingy back street is unpleasant, the child she had given birth to has been taken from her, and she is reduced to the powerless schoolgirl role. Despite being 32 years old at the time, Sheena did not feel grown up enough for the huge and radical change of becoming a mother. The school uniform identifies those who have not had a 'rite of passage' into adulthood.

Sheena contracted German measles early in her pregnancy, not so early that a handicapped baby would be inevitable but not late enough to be certain that it would be unharmed. She had to choose between having a termination and continuing with the pregnancy. She chose to continue, and for the first time in her life defied the medical profession, who were dismayed at her decision.

The nurse with her arms 'piled high with babies' symbolised a casual, almost careless attitude to these bundles of humanity, as it they are inanimate, lifelike 'plastic'. Plastic cannot feel emotions, and Sheena sees the nurse as treating these 'babies' as if they too cannot feel anything. The dream tells us that she felt her possibly damaged child within was viewed by the medical staff who had advocated an abortion as just another one to add to the pile. Sheena is left feeling that she has been a disobedient girl who has gone against the advice of her betters and has been wrong. There is certainly a feeling of 'I told you so' in the last part of the dream.

Sheena's dream allowed her to express her fears and anxieties, but it was not in any way precognitive. She had a perfectly formed daughter, though she did have a period of depression after the birth, probably as a reaction to the stressful experiences encountered during her pregnancy.

LABOUR

Dreams about labour can help the process of giving birth for the first time. Research by Carolyn Winget and Frederick Kapp in the 1970s found that the content of dreams during pregnancy is related to the length of labour. The more anxious the dream content, the more likely the dreamer to have a quick, satisfactory first labour. Winget and Kapp concluded that anxious dreams prepare women for the stresses of childbirth, while women who had long labours were too fearful to allow even symbolic representation to come through in their dreams. By dealing with difficulties in the dreams we are more capable of dealing with them in waking life.

> When I was pregnant I often dreamt that I was in labour. I would be rushed to hospital, where I would give birth. Increasingly in the recurring dream, I found that I was in the dark and had to be woken up to be told I had had the baby. I asked if I could see my baby but I wasn't allowed to although I was assured the baby was all right ... The dream was very significant for, when I did have my baby, I had a Caesarean and didn't see my daughter for many hours because her condition was poor and she was kept in an incubator.' (Tania)

Tania was indeed 'in the dark', anaesthetised and unconscious when her daughter was born.

Sometimes the accuracy of dream details is quite startling.

Karen, a woman in her late twenties, had a dream four weeks before her baby was due:

> I dreamt that there were five midwives round me telling me to push and things like that. I shouted out, 'It's a girl', just as she came out, before they had time to tell me. It was so real that when I woke up I thought I'd had the baby.

Her labour turned out to be just like this. There were five women around her delivery bed, a midwife accompanied by two trainees and two female students, all urging her towards a successful birth. She did shout the sex of her daughter before anyone else had a chance to do so. Karen's dream dealt directly with her delivery, the number of people present and the usual encouragements to push that help in that last hurdle when the baby's head is born, so it was not very extraordinary. You could say it was coincidence that the two, the dream and the actual delivery, were so alike. However, Tricia's dream is less easily explained:

> The last time I was pregnant I wanted to have a boy, as I already had a girl. I dreamt I had given birth to a girl, and because I was so disappointed they swapped it for a boy.

At first, this seems like a wish-fulfilment dream, and that is how Tricia saw it, but the events that followed caused her to recall her 'changeling' dream. When her baby was born he weighed only two pounds and, as Tricia later said, 'they didn't notice his genitals'. When told she had given birth to a girl she felt disappointed but was too worried about the health of the new-born to dwell on unfulfilled wishes for a boy. Some time later an embarrassed nurse came to her as she was sleeping and woke her with the news that she had had a boy after all! 'They had made a mistake because no one had bothered to check his sex,' she told me. 'I often wonder if they did swap or if my dream was preparing me for the mistake.'

Was this dream precognitive? Or was Tricia able to tune into something that was happening to her body of which her conscious mind was unaware? This type of dream is not rare. Once again, it tells us that there is a form of 'knowledge' that we possess but we have generally not learnt to explain or control.

Amrita's account of her first pregnancy

Dreams can be like dress rehearsals for future events. In dreams of pregnancy we rehearse what will happen. Amrita came to England with her husband, a doctor who had accepted a specialist post in a North-West hospital:

> As a first time mother-to-be, a *prima gravida*, I was excited and therefore especially aware of all the differences in me, the changes that came about (both physically and mentally) as a result of the expected baby. Around this time I started becoming aware of how much more vivid were my dreams of home and becoming a mother. In the beginning, when I was still a bit apprehensive and worried about the pregnancy, I'd dream of blood and aborting, disturbing dreams that were a reflection of my waking anxieties. As the baby became an established reality, the content of my dreams changed to dreams of counting to ten and breathing deeply, of having my baby, of having my family in India visit us and of establishing a daily routine in which any baby was a natural part of our lives.

Her dreams acknowledge her anxieties, work through them and give her confidence that all is well. One of the things she hated most about being in England was that both her and her husband's families were in India and could not share in this experience. So she just brought them into the whole event by dreaming them in. Such wish-fulfilment dreams were useful in reducing the normal stresses of pregnancy.

Amrita was plagued by fears of abortion at the start of her pregnancy, and her dreams reflected this. She dreamed of passing blood during urination, and not even the constant reassurances of her doctor, husband and friends could stop these dreams.

> But once the baby was an established reality, so to speak, at about six months, I stopped having these dreams only to dream of going into labour, having contractions, willing myself to relax, going to hospital, celebrating the baby's birth at home in India or seeing my family here with us in Birmingham.

Like so many pregnant women, all her waking anxieties, hopes and wishes were reflected in her dreams. She realised that she never dreamed of having a male child, it was always a girl. Both Amrita and her husband would prefer to have a girl but had prepared themselves to have one of either sex, so she thought. She said:

> My dreams revealed, however, a stubborn subconscious refusal to accept the possibility that I might have a boy. It is only through recording my dreams that I know that if it is a boy, I will find it hard to accept him as whole-heartedly as I would a girl. This may probably help me to avoid rejecting the child when he arrives.

Looking back over her experience, Amrita felt that her dreams did help. They helped to relieve anxieties, and after the baby was born, she said:

> I feel I could put the experience behind me all the quicker because of the joy and anticipation built up by my dreams during my pregnancy. I dreamed only of having a girl baby, a rejection of a male child. When I had worked this out for myself in the later stages of my pregnancy, I was still hoping for a girl, but was ready to consider the possibility of a boy. Without this rational working through of what was a very strong preference, I could have rejected my son when he came along.

Behind the wish to have a girl baby was her need for female company at home. Amrita came from a female-dominated home. The only man around was her father, but she wasn't very close to him. In England her main companion is her husband, and that made her feel that she would be left out in father–son activities. She talked this over with her husband, who comes from a male-dominated home. He told her that all the activity at home revolved around his mother, the only female there. Together they were able to work out her worries. It was her dreams that gave her the insight into her own anxieties.

After the birth

It is a very rewarding experience to have a dream that helps you take that step forward or even pushes you on. Sasha knows that she will turn to her dreams when she needs help.

> After my baby was born, I had a terrible two days when, because of the drugs I had been given, and the pain and discomfort, I seemed to be absolutely 'dry'. The baby would suck and sleep, but I felt I wasn't giving him enough. The third night I dreamt that I was walking in a beautiful garden. There was an elusive perfume in the air, and I was drawn by it and wandered on. Later I came to a beautiful clearing where a bright fountain was spraying the air with that perfume. I walked to it and dipped my hand into it, and then drank some of the liquid. It was sweet. I knew that this was milk. I kept on drinking and got really bloated, and then I woke up. I decided to keep on trying to breastfeed, and finally I got it right.

> The second night after Lucy's arrival I had a vivid dream. I dreamt that I had lain my beautiful little baby on the bed, exactly as I had been accustomed to doing during the day, and then walked across to the corner of the room. As I turned back, I saw Lucy falling off the bed — a very high bed. It was in slow motion, and I watched as she fell on to

> the cold, hard floor beneath. The complete horror of the event left me terrified. I experienced all the implications of it simultaneously ... I felt I already loved her more than anything but was unable to prevent her from being crushed on the floor. I attempted to run towards her and scream, but I was locked in complete paralysis and the dream ended ... After this dream I was most careful to place the baby well away from the edge of the bed.

Though this dream came only two nights after Lucy's birth, it reveals a strong emotional bond and shows the feelings of responsibility that Sue, the mother, had developed. While awake Sue must have noted that laying the baby on the bed could be dangerous, and the dream reinforced the unconscious message, ensuring that the baby was protected from accidental injury.

Just as Sue's dream tells us that major bonding, that emotionally vital join between mother and infant, has taken place, so Natalie's dream demonstrates that she too has formed a strong emotional connection with her new son. She had this dream a few days after the birth of her fourth child:

> I'm suddenly aware that I've lost my baby. He has been taken by an unknown 'them'. The remorse and fear are terrible. Start searching desperately. I'm in a strange town in a strange country. There seems to be a large complex building in yellow stone, like an amusement park. I must try to find him there. They will try to prevent me. Remorse.

In her dream Natalie has become separated; she is horrified at 'losing' him. As mothers we have myriad fears for new-born babies. Will I be able to protect this fragile child from danger? Will I be able to look after my baby? Natalie's subconscious tells her that her essential life-giving relationship will take her into complex areas she has not known before. She will experience a metaphorical 'strange town in a strange country'. These dreams show how the dreamers have accepted their roles as nurturers and protectors of their offspring. Natalie's feeling of 'remorse' concerns an additional issue, one still not discussed widely enough.

Shortly after childbirth, usually a few days later or within a few weeks, there can be a tremendous feeling of sadness. Feelings of anti-climax, loss and misery engulf even as you delight in the new baby. The reality is that the mother has lost, physically, the child she carried inside. She has lost that complete union. The intimacy and ultimate protection her body afforded has gone. The child is separated. While tiredness and hormonal changes play an important role in the sudden mood changes at this time, we need to accept the rightness of tears after birth. Natalie's dream brings out her feelings of loss; it enables her to know her emotions.

Infants are totally dependent on the person who cares for them, usually the mother, and dreams predictably reflect the anxieties attached to such a life-and-death role, as this example shows:

> I had a recurring dream in pregnancy that I had had a baby but forgot about it for several days, so that when I went back to it, it had died of neglect and starvation.

The dream forces home the message that if you, the mother, do not take care of your baby, it will die. Sometimes, though, the 'baby' may be a vulnerable part of you, the dreamer. You may not be caring for yourself properly so your dreams urge you to better self-nurturing. We will examine this more fully later in the book.

Positive dreaming and visualisation

During pregnancy Melinda was determined to practise her breathing exercises and relaxation. She used positive affirmations to prepare herself: 'I will be well and healthy throughout this pregnancy. I will enjoy the birth of my baby as much as possible and it will be normal and relaxed.' In some cases this will stimulate positive dreams. The 'healthy' suggestions worked tremendously well. She was fitter than ever before. She had the 'perfect pregnancy', as her doctor kept saying. Melinda said:

> The birth itself was perfect too — a short labour even though Lois is my only child, and she was born without complications only moments after starting to push, exactly as I'd imagined it to be. A nurse said she'd never seen breathing techniques so well applied and asked me how I did it!

Melinda's dreams while asleep at night were often on the subject of babies and birth.

The development of dreams during pregnancy

Most women dream a lot more than usual during pregnancy. The alteration in sleeping patterns caused by physical changes is one reason, and disturbance by foetal movements in the later stages another. More important, perhaps, are the psychological causes. Dreams during pregnancy show how women learn to handle and resolve fears about pregnancy and childbirth, and their recall helps us to adapt to the stress of childbirth itself. These dreams also help in the process of accommodating all the new knowledge and experiences we have at the time. During the final period of pregnancy, dreams seem to be inner rehearsals for what is to come. Rosie's dream diary documents such changes:

> In this vivid dream I found myself to be very pregnant and in labour. Everything seemed pleasant and painless at this point. I was in a corridor close to an adjoining office with a large door and an open window revealing a panoramic view of the office interior — a desk, filing cabinets and a large, cold marble slab of a table. In the next instant Kev, my husband, was ordered away from me and I was put on the table/slab and slashed with a knife. There was a lot of blood about, and I remembered telling Kev in the dream that this wasn't how I wanted it to be. I think I remember getting a baby also. It sounds like a nightmare, but it wasn't really; my

> feelings were definitely disgruntled about Kev going away, but yet acceptance also that things would have to be done before the baby was born.

She also dreamt of giving birth to a deformed baby, then she had another dream:

> In another I dreamt about seeing the baby who was coming. This dream occurred in the latter stages of my pregnancy, and in it my child appeared as a tiny, delicate, skinny black-haired little mite, fragile and extraordinarily beautiful. She was so lovely in this dream that it felt to be one of the happiest dreams I had ever experienced. These happy feelings remained with me for days, and I told it to everyone. It was a tremendous booster, I just wanted to have the baby then. Everyone hoped my dream baby would resemble my real baby, and as things turned out she did. Anna was almost exactly like her.

Rosie felt that her dreams helped her towards having a 'perfect birth' — a short labour and no complications, even though she was her first child. Her earlier dreams showed an acceptance that birth might not be a trouble-free experience, but she is reconciled to that and goes on to produce a healthy daughter.

Other dreams of pregnancy

Meg suffered great personal tragedy. She learnt, through a dream, that all was not well with her baby:

> My first son was stillborn. I remember very clearly, a couple of months before his birth, dreaming of a baby boy lying on top of a table, but I could never reach him. I knew without doubt that he was my baby, but I would never hold him.

Maybe, like Tricia, Meg was reacting to subliminal messages from her body. At one level she knew that there were development problems that caused her child to be at risk.

Avril, a student I taught recently, wondered if her dreams were a response to an abnormality already present in the foetus, which later caused a cot death. Her dreams during pregnancy were quite different from the ones she had while carrying her two healthy daughters:

> The dreams began very soon after the confirmation of my pregnancy and were quite frequent, once or twice a week. Usually it was the same dream: a tiny white coffin, masses of flowers and a beautiful baby boy lying inside the open coffin ... It always appeared to be in slow motion and to last a long time, although I can't remember anything else happening.

These dreams were extremely upsetting, though Avril tried not to dwell on them. However, she also had another dreadful recurring dream. She dreamt that she was going into labour screaming that something was wrong. Again, it appeared to be in slow motion, and the screaming would go on and on until the dream clouded and she knew she was dying. At that point she woke up.

Even during her waking hours Avril felt morbid, filled with a terrible sense of foreboding, although the pregnancy was fine and she was physically very well. When Mark was born, he was a perfectly normal healthy boy, but she still felt that things weren't right. The dream with the white coffin continued right up until a week before Avril found Mark dead at four and a half months. Since that sudden cot death Avril has never had the dream again.

Three years after the tragic death of her son, Avril still feels his loss very deeply. Her dreams, she felt, were warning her, preparing her for the agonising reality of burying her son in his tiny coffin. The peculiar slow-motion quality is mentioned by other women who have had such dreams. Maybe one day, obstetricians and others concerned with attending pregnant women will routinely ask about dreams and use them to investigate and improve their ante- and post-natal care.

THE MENOPAUSE

Amy, aged 43, has begun to notice that after many years of sparse dreaming, her dreams are becoming more insistent. They are easier to recall; indeed, they seem to demand recall though at times she fights against it. Not too happy with the changes that are happening to her body, she is loath to talk to others about 'the change', and this reluctance surfaces during sleep.

Amy dreams of dead people and about being in dissecting rooms filled with bodies on slabs. As she walks around, she is terrified that she might accidentally touch one, for in some way this will taint her. She has no waking experience of such places, and no-one close to her is ill or has died recently. So do these dreams reflect her psyche coming to terms with ageing and accepting that parts of herself are ending, particularly her fertility? Again, the dream setting is important: a room where minute, detailed examination takes place, where students learn about how people are made and what constitutes physical reality. It is a place of life and death, and Amy needs somehow to 'learn' about this even though she is scared. What dissection does Amy have to do in order to understand herself better?

Like many women at this stage in life, she feels low. Her children have grown up, left home and lead lives that do not involve her. She was always 'just a housewife', devoting her skills to child-rearing and homemaking, and now there seems little point in her existence. Pauline Bart, a psychologist who has written about depression in middle-aged women, found that such feelings sprang from lack of self-esteem rather than from hormonal changes of the menopause; as she says, 'There's no bar mitzvah for menopause.'

Ann Mankowitz echoes this view and explains how such feelings are revealed in dreams. In *Change of Life: A Study in Dreams of the Menopause*, she shows how they reflect the way the menopause is unsympathetically treated in our society; it carries none of the significance of other 'rites of passage', such as marriage or childbirth, and no-one marks it in any way. This may well be because it is seen as the end of a woman's creative, reproductive cycle. Most women have spent more than thirty years, apart from pregnancies or ill health, living with a monthly cycle that confirms their potential to create new life. The creative force is there even though the woman may not bear children. When the cycle stops, that power is taken away and we need time to come to terms with its loss.

As long as women continue to be defined largely by the functions of the uterus, the menopause will be a difficult time for us. I cannot think of any advertisements, television or radio programmes or popular literature that deal in a helpful way with issues raised by the menopause. Like incest, it is still a taboo area.

> After years of sparse dreaming, I now seem to be dreaming more. I think there is a connection with the 'change of life' approaching as I'm 45 now.

As a woman undergoes the change of life at menopause, dreams reflect new dimensions and can reveal new paths for this important, often transformative and creative time of life. It is to that creativity that we now turn.

CHAPTER 7

VENUS AND THE CREATIVE SPARK

I dream for a living.

Steven Spielberg

The idea of creation is at the heart of what it means to be human. All of us have the capacity and a deep desire to bring into existence that which was not there before. This may come in the form of giving birth to an idea, making an object such as a sculpture, a painting or a poem. In *Time Magazine* in 1985 US film director and producer Steven Spielberg gave praise for the power of dreaming. He later named his production company 'Dreamworks'. Dreams are the creative spark that enrich life in so many ways. Whether it is painting, writing, storytelling or problem-solving, dreams can be your inspiration.

In the search through our vast memory store, the brain makes bizarre links, and this creates weird dreams. As we sleep, we're busy exploring connections between old and new memories. As the neuroscientist Robert Stickgold said of sleep and dreams: 'When I think about how I would design a brain, I would want it to stop and look for distant associations. This is what most people would call creativity.' It's a view that Sara agrees with:

> My dreams put me in touch with my intuition rather than my logic. The juxtaposition of people, images and situations often sparks off new ideas in me.
>
> Dreams put me in touch with something undefined but which feels very important and give freer reign to my imagination and feeling than is possible in everyday life.

Noted American dream researcher Kelley Bulkeley said at the

1999 Association for the Study of Dreams conference: 'Dreaming provokes creative consciousness.' We know this is true for many gifted scientists who have dreamed of radical solutions to seemingly intractable puzzles.

Dreams don't come to tell you what you already know, they break new ground, bring new insights and invite you to increase your creative response to the world. And creativity is not merely about having new ideas, it can also be a life saver. It can be the means by which we escape depression, mental illness or social inadequacy.

INSPIRATIONAL DREAMS

> The prerequisite of originality is the art of forgetting for the moment what we know. Hence the importance of the unconscious who puts reason to sleep and restores for a moment the innocence of vision.
>
> *Arthur Koestler*

In the uncensored state of dreaming, startling and original ideas arise that bring innovative music, artwork, writing or new ways of relating to your world.

In *Living on the Edge*, Elizabeth Wilde MacCormick tells of a powerful dream. She dreamt that she was running along the cliff edge in Suffolk, where she lived next to the North Sea. Something tapped her right shoulder. Impatiently, she brushed it off and rushed on. This happened again, then after the third time she turned around. She saw a young man with a kind face standing behind her. He was pushing a lifeless young woman in a wheelchair. The dream continued. The young man said that all they wanted was permission to put up the woman's easel. The dream ended there, but Elizabeth knew it was a numinous dream, and this guide in the shape of a young man was telling her something profound.

> I knew, in my head, that I had not given enough time to the 'artist' within. But the potency of the dream's intent was only fully revealed to me when I actually had to live body and soul 'on the edge', reclaiming the energies of these two inner young masculine and feminine figures who had come calling.

In June 1992, one month after the dream, Elizabeth was diagnosed as suffering from viral meningitis, encephalitis and labyrinthitis, which took her to — and beyond — the edge for the next two and a half years. Her book tells of this journey and reaffirms the significance of her dream.

Dreams can be inspirational, as many artists know. But what is inspiration? The word 'inspiration' means to 'breathe life into'. Artists record inspiring dreams and bring them to life in words, pictures or music. Dream diaries certainly spark off ideas for writing, painting and other forms of creative work.

Dark men dreams

In her inspirational book, *Women Who Run With The Wolves*, Clarissa Pinkola Estes writes of 'dark men dreams'. These are dreams that come to women, and men too, when creativity is ignored and feature thugs, rapists and prowlers who threaten them, steal from them and do far worse things. We have seen these in trauma dreams, she says: 'But most often they are dreams of women who are drying out, who are not giving care to the instinctual side of their lives, who steal from themselves, deprive the creative function, and sometimes make no effort to help themselves.' Susan, knows this kind of dream:

> I have a recurring nightmare where a dark figure, sometimes draped in a dark cloak, enters the bedroom and gets closer and closer until it is looming over me. Usually the face is indistinguishable but sometimes it is male, sometimes female. As it gets closer I feel terror and sometimes call out.

> I wake up before it harms me. I have often woken and continued to see it for a few seconds.

The *animus*, the 'soul force', the masculine force in women, helps women to act on their own behalf in the world, to be assertive, to stick up for themselves. The *anima* in men's dreams helps them to express the more intuitive, nurturing aspect of their psyche, the part that can be spontaneously creative in a more lyrical, less analytic fashion.

Dreams are entrances, access points to the next stage in the process of developing awareness. They are 'wake-up' calls to the next step on the path of individuation. Sometimes we need their push in order to truly take off.

> We took them to the edge and bade them fly.
> They held on.
> 'Fly,' we said. They held on.
> We pushed them over the edge.
> And they flew.
>
> *Guillaume Apollinaire*

WRITERS' INSPIRATION

Edna O'Brien, the very successful Irish novelist, wonders at our capacity for amazing dreams of imagination and creative fertility. She said: 'There's a quotation of Yeats's that says: "In dreams begin responsibilities." I would have called it self-knowledge. That sleeping side of the psyche ... is so fertile and so full of surprises and solutions.' When we are awake it is easy to ignore the creative potential of our dreaming selves. O'Brien goes on to say in 'Me and My Psyche': 'It's ironic, though, that when we are awake we are often asleep and that many people's most aware and heightened time is when they are asleep.' If you want to maximise your 'heightened time', keep your dream journal. In valuing your dreams you nourish your creative streak.

> I use my dreams frequently when writing prose as my dreams are so vivid. It is like watching a film playing before you, calling out to be written and shared.

The writer Robert Louis Stevenson, when at a loss for a solution to something that puzzled or disturbed him would confidently assert: 'Never mind, we shall have it at seven o'clock tomorrow morning.' 'Sleeping on it' was a popular idea even in his day, and he knew his dream muses — his 'brownies', as he called them — would bring him ideas for plots for his books as well as solve problems for him. His idea for *Dr Jekyll and Mr Hyde* came in a dream, and he said he had to do little other than write the story down because it was presented from beginning to end.

Writers love their dreams; as Thea describes:

> Although I lead a very busy life, I also lead a very busy dream life! I really love my dream world — I say world because the places, the people, the situations in my dreams I can almost call up to order. I know the places I visit are places I knew well in my childhood, but they are exaggerated, larger than life, almost as if painted by Dali! I also dream in colour, and remember one dream in particular where I was standing in a field and looking at a range of mountains in the distance. The sky was a deep blue and the mountains incredibly green. Another time I had made a plane journey to some island with my son. The sands on the beach were yellow, the sea very blue and the sunshine very intense. On other occasions, I have been lost, or wandering alone, at night. The countryside is always very dark and the lights of houses, buses, cars, very bright.
>
> What I do find, though, is that whereas I could once claim to have a vivid imagination — I make a living from writing — since the dreams took hold all that has vanished. I wish it would return, though not at the expense of losing my dreams. My dream experiences open a door into another world.

Or Isabelle Allende:

> As a writer I accept everything is possible: layers of truth and belief and the subjective — dreams, coincidences, fears, obsessions. All that gives texture to writing.

A present-day writer, Debbie Freedman, told me of the importance of dreams in her creative life:

> I came to Manchester in 1977, with three toddlers and a paediatrician husband, who worked days and nights, saving lives. Distancing myself from parents and sisters for the first time in my life, I was determined to do something useful — as well as trying to become a writer. If it involved night work, all the better. I applied to be a Samaritan. I had good interpersonal skills, and an instinctive empathy with desperate people. But the Samaritans rejected me. I wrote asking if they might give their reasons for the rejection — they refused. I was profoundly hurt.
>
> I had a dream in which the decision was reversed. A trained Samaritan now, I was called at midnight to accompany someone on an emergency suicide mission. I ran down a dark street, looking for 'the desperate person'. We came to a large block of flats. I ran up and down staircases, knocking on locked doors, trying to locate the crying woman I could now dimly hear. Suddenly I noticed two shadowy figures in a doorway. My parents were standing there — silently watching.
>
> I woke up feeling elated and moved. I now had a radio play to write. I called it 'The Bad Samaritan'. At the end of my play, my protagonist understood that the crying woman in the dream was her. She phoned the Samaritans again — this time as a client. But I had moved on. I had become a writer.

'The Bad Samaritan' was directed in Manchester by Kay Patrick, and broadcast in Thirty-Minute Theatre on BBC Radio Four in 1983.

Clearly, this dream was very important for Debbie. I asked her how dreams help her creativity. She said:

> Firstly, I feel my dreams help me in a creative way by taking me to a place where there are no barriers, judgements, conditioning, or limitations. I am a totally free being in my dreamlife, and in turn this opens up the creative/intuitive side of me/my brain.

When the censor is absent fresh, innovative creations emerge. She is not alone. Anna develops the theme:

> I'm glad of them, and only wish I remembered more of them. A particularly good dream makes me feel more potent, it's almost like a proof of inner life at times when my faith in the vitality of my imagination is at an ebb.

Many writers and poets have problems with addiction, and many write as a way of exorcising demons. Julia, a recovering alcoholic, had this prescient dream when she was 16:

> I dreamt I was bent like an old woman and tottering down long corridors to get a drink of alcohol. I woke and immediately wrote a poem in the dark: "I was a little old lady, Yes, dipso, dipso, I was a little old lady who drank all day, I was gone far out of my mind," it began. It was quite a long poem and I've never altered it. When I went to live in London at 18 it all came true. I became a raving alcoholic and lost my health within a matter of months.

Your dreams as problem-solving tools

In many of the Venus myths we meet creative responses to difficult problems. Like Ariadne, who spins a golden thread so that Theseus can escape from the labyrinth and the minotaur, our dreams can show us how to avoid danger and resolve difficulties.

> I feel my dreams are essential to my unravelling the 'mysteries' of life. Dreams are a tool, and it is necessary for each and every one of us to become aware and familiar with symbolism in order to utilise dreams properly. Universal symbolism for a higher purpose and personal symbolism for a more basic approach.

For the last two centuries scientists have suggested that there are links between dreams and memory, that memories become consolidated as you dream. In doing this, problems we have grappled with during waking hours often become resolved as we sleep. Robert Stickgold, a neuroscientist at Harvard Medical School, goes further and says that deep sleep and REM dream sleep cycles are vital for absorbing information, for finding patterns in our memories and for learning and improving skills. In the article 'Perchance to Dream' (published in 1999) he states emphatically his belief that certain aspects of learning cannot happen without sleep: 'Even if I'm not conscious of it, I always "sleep on a problem" and have usually found a simple solution by the next morning.'

So, while we slumber we continue to learn and carry on working out solutions to problems. Without REM sleep our ability to absorb new material is affected, we perform poorly and complete tasks more slowly. While we dream, we are hard at work finding the links between old and new memories, which is why we have dreams where an old friend or a place we used to live suddenly appear in a present-day setting. These connections are important and necessary for problem-solving. Even nightmares can be useful:

> Nightmares are always helpful because sometimes when things are getting me down I refuse to think about them consciously, but the nightmares force me to think about

> them and work out what they mean and do something about it all, because they don't stop until I do.

Look back at your childhood dreams — often dreams from childhood give clues to issues and experiences that may still cause you concern now, though you may not be aware of it consciously.

> I have a fairly frequent dream about clinging on to something such as a bar, or cliff top at great height — very frightening. Just recently I decided in a dream that I was fed up with this and decided to let go and find out what would happen. I incurred a slight bump on the head and slightly damaged feelings about my family watching me, but I can remember sort of philosophically accepting the experience and thinking, 'well, that wasn't too bad'.

In his book *Phantoms in the Brain: Human Nature and the Architecture of the Mind*, V.S. Ramachandran describes the Indian genius Ramujan. Ramujan had not had any formal mathematical education, yet his ability to solve intractable problems and devise new theorems was remarkable. When asked how he could do such breathtaking creative maths, he explained that the fully formed equations were whispered to him in dreams by the village deity Goddess Namagiri.

A woman living in London also meets unusual people in her dreams:

> In my dreams there are people that I do not know in real life, but are recurrent 'dream people'. If I am deprived of dream sleep and therefore dreams, I hallucinate. My dreams often give me inspiration as a writer and artist, my professions, but they can often solve problems by giving an example or by showing me someone from my waking life, for what they are underneath their facade. My 'dream people' are often instrumental in showing me clues I have missed.

These creative guides will help if you let them. Many years ago, when I had begun writing but wasn't sure if my work was good enough to be published, I had a reassuring 'guide' dream. I found myself in the library at Manchester University, being taken through various rooms, past shelves of books, until we arrived at the psychology of dreams section. There, my guide simply showed me that there was a space where my books could go. I still feel a surge of warmth and gratitude for that dream, as I sit and write this, my eighth book.

Playing with words

The language of dreams includes plays on words, particularly puns. There are verbal puns in which words that sound the same, as in the case of 'pale' and 'pail', or puns based on reversals, visual puns, puns based on proper names, slang metaphors and puns related to common body language. For example, one woman dreamt that, while working as a waitress, she was 'shot over a trifle'. The dream customer had asked for a trifle for his dessert, but on waking the dreamer knew the trifle really related to a minor difficulty at work, which was growing out of all proportion. By being amusing or unusual in their juxtapositioning of images, these dreams grab our attention and give us food for — waking — thought.

In her excellent book, *The Dream* Game, Ann Faraday described the intense mental activity, that background 'chatter', which continues as we sleep: 'Metaphors, slang, puns, overlapping meanings and figures of speech are the language used by the chattering mind to create new forms of mental life, of which the dream is only one.' She gave an example of a verbal pun that might be seeing a man in a 'gilt' uniform, where it really related to feelings of 'guilt'.

Pavanne has recurring dreams of climbing a steep cliff where there is nothing for her to 'hang on to'. Invariably it is dark, which is a way of saying she feels 'in the dark' about her future. In this dream which Faraday describes, Lottie recognises she prefers not to 'reveal' herself:

> I had a dream about choosing between two dresses. One was very revealing and the other was just smart. They were both in vivid, silky material, and I was trying them on in front of a mirror. I wanted the first one to begin with because it was my favourite colour, until I realised how revealing it was.

Body language also provides us with many metaphors. Dreaming of a skeleton might indicate that you need to get down to the 'bare bones' of some situation. Pam dreamt she was spinning out of control, while in waking life she is in a spin — too much to do and taking on too many commitments. Others who dream of flying but can hardly get off the ground, have problems 'taking off'; gravity, possibly symbolising a too serious attitude, pulls them down.

Dreams use slang or colloquial metaphors to reveal our internal emotional landscape:

> I once had a dream where everything was pink. The clothes I wore, the cars, the house and even the trees and grass were pink.

Kirsty was feeling 'in the pink' when she had this dream. Whenever Winnie was incubating a fever as a child, she dreamt of a steamroller coming towards her. The heat of her fever is connected with the 'steam', and she felt flattened and rolled over by her illness when it knocked her off her feet.

Liza spoke of a recurring dream, in which she was 'climbing a wall with a man — horizontally'. This dream felt very spiritual, she said; and she thought it might be linked to the deep spiritual relationship she had with her married lover, who was having a 'rest' from her. Perhaps a simpler, more prosaic interpretation would have been more accurate — that the relationship was driving her 'up the wall' — and she was lying down and taking it.

Here is another dream in which the language is quite revealing:

> I dreamt I was walking around in bare feet and I noticed that on my foot I had a toe missing. It had been cut out from my foot. I thought about this and then realised that having a missing toe affected my balance and I felt 'off balance'. I had a gut feeling that it related to my relationship with a friend. I felt that somehow I needed to cut her out of my life as my toe had been cut out (but would I then be unbalanced or find my balance in a new way?). But the end result was that I thought long and hard about our relationship and eventually did pull away from her, and felt much better for doing it. It was a huge step forward for me.

She needed to 'cut out' the offending relationship and find new balance. It was a life-transforming dream.

Claudia's mother had one of her 'howlers', as the family called them:

> She dreamt that I was a small child. I am 31 now, and she tucked me up in, not my cot, but her roasting tin of all things. She made sure I was comfortable and then put me in the oven and switched it on. Half an hour later she came to check me to see if I was 'done'. There I was in the roasting tin with fat red cheeks and sweat pouring off me — she said I was basting nicely.

She wondered if this dream was anything to do with the central heating, which was constantly on full. Claudia said she couldn't stop laughing at her dream, though her mother seemed rather upset by it.

Some dreams of sex are metaphors, symbolising feelings of attraction, intimacy or connection with others. Yvette, the owner of a London art gallery, told me:

> I once went to a Freudian analyst. He decided that my disaster-filled, travelling-to-important events and always-being-late dreams were a result of an inability to orgasm. You

> know, never being able to get 'there', never achieving the 'aim'. However, now I can orgasm my little socks off and I still have those dreams! So I searched for another meaning, and have decided that, at least partially, these dreams represent an innate fear of failure.

Other people's interpretations, whether they be friend or Freud, are not necessarily right. If the interpretation does not resonate, does not feel right to you, then continue to work on the meaning yourself.

Fiona dreams:

> I am being chased by my father and there is an undercurrent, usually sexual. In another I am vainly trying to find space in my childhood home. All the doors and cupboards are ajar and I don't have any room for myself.

'Space' means much more the physical space — it can symbolise privacy, room for emotional distance, and indicate a place where there are boundaries so that others keep far enough away. Notice how Fiona is trying to find 'space'. The doors are 'ajar'. One meaning of 'jar' means conflict or clash of interests, which aptly sums up her childhood situation.

Cars and travelling are frequent dream metaphors. The passengers who travel with you in dreams reveal dynamics of relationships. Pat's dreams show her anxiety:

> I am driving a car with my mother as passenger. I suddenly get afraid because I have no driving licence or insurance and have not passed my driving test. I stop the car, afraid that the police will find out. I have to ring my husband to come and drive the car home.

Pat's lack of confidence means she has to ask her husband to rescue her. She is afraid of being caught, though nothing actually happens. She is progressing quite well when panic hits and immobilises her. Her own comments are revealing:

> I have wondered if the dream about driving could mirror feelings of guilt at doing something that I know is wrong, and they make me stop the car. I suppose deep down I feel guilty about doing my degree away from home. I come home at weekends. People are always surprised that my husband doesn't mind. I also feel guilty at times because I love my husband as a brother, not a husband. On many occasions when I have dreamt about myself, I don't recognise myself.

She feels her place is with her husband, even though, she says, he does not object to her studying for her degree at a distant university. The dream, however, uncovers much more. She feels guilt because she has no authority to do this — 'no licence', no protection in the form of 'insurance' and no qualifications: 'she has not passed the test'. Suddenly she feels inadequate, incapable and scared of her independent actions. In the dream, symbolically Pat resumes dependence on her husband. What she associates with the dream, her fraternal feelings towards her husband, tell us that Pat has some difficult issues to resolve before she can accept her self. Her 'car' dream drives her towards facing these issues.

Creativity

> What lies behind us and what lies in front of us are tiny matters, compared with what lies within us.
>
> *Ralph Waldo Emerson*

There are many paths to creativity, and the images that arise in dreams are one source of inspiration.

> Some years ago my godfather had to design a casket for Canterbury Cathedral. He was stuck for a design and dozed off in the sun. He dreamt and woke up to find himself

> doodling, and that was the design for the casket. It is still there in the cathedral.

These dreams give insights into the unconscious; they make the unconscious visible to us. They should be treated gently and handled with respect.

Our creative side longs to be fed. Recent studies have shown that people who regularly attend concerts, theatre, art exhibitions and other cultural and community events have greater life expectancy than those who do not. In fact, one study said that not going to such cultural events was more dangerous than being a heavy smoker! The social aspect, the sense of community, of sharing with other people, is vital, as is the feeding of our innate creativity. This part of each of us needs to be stimulated. If we fail to look after this part of our nature the ultimate outcome may be a weakened immune system. As we know from Candace Pert's *Molecules of Emotion*, where we fail to acknowledge psychological needs, we are more susceptible to illness.

Rehearsal dreams

Dreams let us try out various hypothetical situations that might completely throw us off balance if we tried them out in waking life. They give us a 'virtual reality' simulation, using thoughts and actions normally eclipsed by the conscious mind. Repressed memories and thoughts that are 'out of bounds' appear in dreams. As a leading brain researcher, Dr V.S. Ramachandran, says: 'Unmasking such memories during dreams may permit a realistic and emotionally charged situation to take place while preventing the penalties that would result if you were to do this when awake.'

> I dream of situations where I am standing up for myself and know that this is because I am too reserved during waking hours, but I feel it helps me sort out situations sometimes or they just help me get rid of pent-up feelings of animosity.

Dreams often act as confidence boosters in all sorts of ways and let us experiment with activities we have not previously considered. This includes sexual activity:

> Usually in dreams sex seems much better than in real life. Sometimes I try to remember the little details that made it so good to put them into practice next time, but it never seems to work out the same, more's the pity.

Aimee's wistful yearnings, characteristic of the idealisations referred to earlier, are not met in waking life, for, as she continues, in dreams:

> I get swept off my feet by a man and it ends up in a situation, not usually in bed. Exotic things I wouldn't normally do, as I would be too embarrassed, but perhaps if I tried it would be better — but then dreams are supposed to be better than real life, aren't they? This is the whole thing about dreaming, I think, yearning for things we don't get out of life.

Hannah dreams of her boyfriend, Lee, constantly:

> He is in his early twenties, like me, and I've been seeing him for about three months. He has been in nearly all my dreams for the last two months. Quite often we are making love, although we haven't yet in real life.

In her dreams she can respond to her inner drives even though she has not done so in waking life. It may not be long before she does so because her repetitive dreams are insistent and, as she says herself, 'We haven't made love *yet*', indicating that there may be changes ahead.

Dreams monitor changes in confidence and the resolution of fears, as Pippa explains:

> All my early sexual dreams were ones of terror and attack by

> giant snakes and burglars with knives. Over the years fears have been eliminated and I have pleasurable sensations. For example, I am dressed in silk. A man in a fur coat makes loves to me, the textures are very sensuous. They've helped me change from being sexually afraid to being sexually responsive.

Visual artists

Dali, Picasso, Blake and Paula Rego are all famous painters whose dreams inspired astonishing works of art. The Surrealists deliberately set out to combine the bizarre juxtapositioning of images that occur in dreams to capture the mystery of the unconscious. The artist and visionary William Blake regularly dreamt of his dead brother Robert, who came to help him. In one dream he gave William step-by-step directions for a unique technique to produce luscious colour illustrations, a technique that has only recently been rediscovered.

In many cultures dreams are used to underpin creative processes. In Liberia in Africa traditional Gola artists believe a particular relationship exists between craftwork, dreams and spirit beings. Singers, musicians, woodcarvers and weavers are referred to as dreamers. Each one believes that he has a personal spirit inspirer, to whom his works are attributed and with whom he has a special friendship. The inspiration occurs during the dream experience, which moulds his work, as well as his personality and behaviour.

Marion Silverbear has set up an alternative greeting card company in America that sells cards based on her dreams. 'For me', she says, 'dreams are life itself ... The raw stuff of being creative, wild yet carrying a story consistent over time.' The 'Dream Vestibules', as she calls these stories, represent her life and are full of archetypes. Even the unwanted images are embraced and transformed into arresting images such as 'Inviting the Bums to Tea', 'Painting Myself in a Corner' and 'Baby Eagle Needs His Own Nest'.

Shirin, who has been in a dream-sharing group with a number of women over several years, uses many of the techniques described in Chapter 2. Each year she now makes a calendar based on dream themes that have arisen. She said: 'Nourish your dreams and your dream will nourish you. I get a lot of creative inspiration from my dreams and so much self-understanding. They are the key to self-development.' She passes this on in the calendars she gives to friends and family.

SACRED ART

Meinrad Craighead is an artist from Albuquerque, New Mexico. She built her studio herself, and on each wall she has constructed an altar to goddesses from different traditions: Kwan Yin, Crow Mother, Shakti, Artemis and the Egyptian canine spirit Anubis. Images of birth and life, pomegranates and bleeding wombs, animal companions, moons and trees and eggs are gathered together for her spiritual and artistic practice. She leads four-day creative retreats to explore their archetypal images in art, particularly women's sacred art

Once a nun at Stanbrook Abbey, in England, Meinrad had a spiritual experience that changed her life. She 'heard rushing water inside my body. It didn't alarm me at all. With it came the immediate understanding that this was God inside me, and furthermore that God was Mother — this water inside me was Mother.' In her book *The Mother's Songs: Images of God the Mother*, Meinrad recounts this and explains how she felt led to devote her life to work as a creative visionary. She includes in it shamanic and mythological imagery and the Divine Feminine.

Jung says that whatever it is that fascinates you means that your soul is picking up signals, a sort of vibration or resonance, about the next step to take you on your journey. This creative journey may take the most unusual paths but by tuning into it you will develop greater peace and awareness. Meinrad Craighead is adamant about the importance of dreams and insists we all have the potential for creative image-making. As she says in Allegra

Taylor's delightful book, *I Fly Out With Bright Feathers*: 'We do it every night when we dream.' We might not make clay models or paint dream images but the potential is always there, the creative imagination fed by the great storehouse of memory is always there.

> Everything we experience falls into some kind of centrifugal force which is always moving in us. We remember things which have stuck to the wall and rise up at will when we're writing or painting or dreaming. The rest is forced to the bottom but that doesn't mean it is lost. Its energy acts like a composting material, a deep inner fertilisation. It's all inside us waiting for space and silence, waiting for solitude and encouragement — things that women often lack — in order to emerge.

Sometimes dreams of the deceased can lead us to greater creativity. As psychologist Gayle Delaney points out in her book, *In Your Dreams*, a man called Mr Fischer revealed that a complete psychological technique for a process to work through early parental conflict was presented to him in a dream by Mr Hoffman, deceased. The Fischer–Hoffman process is now widely used in America to help resolve problematic early relationships.

Archetypes

Jung introduced the term 'archetype' to explain the inherited images that arise spontaneously in dreams and daydreams, and come from the deep, unconscious parts of ourselves. They appear in all cultures, and have done so since man drew on the walls of caves. We share a collective unconscious with all mankind, and archetypes of the goddess, the wise man, the shadow and many more come to us as we sleep. They also show up in myths, fairy stories, soap operas and films. Archetypes are particularly apparent in 'big' dreams, the ones that seem impossible to forget. They feel as if they come from a higher source, a wiser being that is timeless.

There is a level of the psyche which operates in images. This is below the level of conscious thinking. Events occur in these deeper recesses and faculties which are rarely touched by the conscious mind. For these faculties, time is no barrier, and the limitations of our personal view of the world and of our self are removed. In this way it is possible to know things we are unaware of in waking life. This sort of knowledge or insight is encoded in a from of images as it approaches the level of conscious thought. Interpreting such meaningful dream-images requires understanding of the language of symbol, it needs clarity and honesty. Images are never important in themselves — only the meaning, and this has to be made by the individual dreamer.

A typical archetype symbol is the wise woman, whom we have already met. She embodies women's magical powers and her connections with nature. Sometimes she seems threatening, often because she wants us to change or is about to inflict change on us whether we want it or not. Gianne felt that her fate was sealed in this dream:

> We then look outside to where a group of small girls are playing games. They turn around and I realise they are dangerous. They come towards our house and we know we will be eaten by them. They all stare. I look up at the house opposite, and in the top room an old woman is spinning. I know she is directing these children. I think 'she is spinning the web of my fate'. I force myself awake.

Like Ariadne, the old woman is spinning. She has girls, immature females, who threaten the dreamer. Perhaps they indicate that some part of her femaleness is still undeveloped, that she needs to act if this part is not to be killed. 'Witches' were, and still are, none other than wise women who preserve in the collective unconscious the remnants of an older religion based on worship of nature and the feminine principle.

In other dreams we meet the 'wise man'. Over twenty years ago I met some characters who are only known to me in my dreams. One of these is the gardener, an old man who seems to know my questions even before I ask. He is always caring and helpful and is a great source of power. Until I recorded my dreams I wasn't aware of him, or other archetypes who appeared, just as I wasn't aware of the patterns in my dream themes. I am still building up my personal dream dictionary, and it becomes richer the more dream work I do. I know that the gardener is a guide who comes to reassure me, and the animals that appear are to do with my wild side and tamed side — but more of that later when you will discover how to understand and interpret your own dreams.

We will spend more time with archetypes in the next chapter when we visit 'Venus and the Dark Shadow'.

CHAPTER 8

VENUS AND THE DARK SHADOW

Those who lose dreaming are lost.

Australian Aboriginal proverb

Dreams reflect the emotions we harbour in the deepest recesses of our soul and psyche. They show up our strength, our weakness, our tenderness and our viciousness. It is very difficult to own those rotten, selfish, miserly, grudging parts of own character that are easy to recognise in other people. For women, accepting the violent, angry aspect of ourselves can be a problem. In nightmares, we face the shadow of ourselves and meet the shadow side of our communities, that dark threat that lurks in the heart of our world wherever we live. In this chapter we discover what we can do to heal the shadow side.

We all contain dark and light. When something comes from the shadow part of ourselves, it doesn't mean that the caring, loving, wonderful side of us isn't still there, merely that it has been masked by the darkness of the shadow. But what is the shadow? How do we define it? The shadow is an archetype that represents the mysterious, often threatening, aspects of our unseen selves. Facing the shadow is the catalyst for personal and spiritual growth. It often leads to a reconnection with intuition. Resistance to it increases tension, whereas acceptance eases it. It is your choice — you can survive and you can decide to thrive.

The shamanistic view of life is that we exist in a web that touches everyone. Sometimes, when something 'big' happens, it shakes all of it, for instance, the death of Diana Princess of Wales, John F. Kennedy or Martin Luther King. Reverberations are felt on many different levels all around the world and are recounted on anniversaries.

> We are the flow, we are the ebb,
> We are the weavers, we are the web.
>
> *Allegra Taylor*

Nightmare shadows

In earlier societies, and still in some today, it was thought that nightmares were the result of some outside force visiting and tormenting the dreamer. The 'nightmare' was the night demon who came to taunt and punish. This stuff of nightmares includes the dreamer being attacked, threatened, trapped and tortured. Possibly the worst nightmare is one in which the dreamer dies.

Not only do we wake up feeling extremely upset, perhaps sobbing, but we may have to accept that our mood is influenced all day, if not longer. Today, we are more likely to recognise that nightmares are triggered by disturbing waking events, worry, stress or personal conflicts. Drugs, medication, alcohol, high temperature and media violence also play their part. Essentially, if you are disturbed you will have disturbing dreams. New challenges, changes in relationships, having a baby or increased responsibilities all have the potential to increase stress and therefore lead to higher levels of anxiety. It really depends on the intensity of the demand for readjustment. In turn, these may provoke nocturnal nightmares, and in cases where acute anxiety develops, it may lead to depression, as we saw in Chapter 5.

Faceless fear

The shadow side of fear is sometimes represented by faceless, anonymous figures. This reveals that we have not yet been able to identify and 'face' whatever it is that is bothering us. For Sylvie, the setting was her vehicle:

> I am in a car. There are faceless people in the dream too, who get out of the car, but I am left as it starts to roll off the cliff. As I am falling I seem to be able to feel my heart start beating faster, but before I reach the ground I awake, crying.

Everyone deserts her and no-one cares for her welfare. She is isolated and only avoids knowing the outcome by the tears of despair that wake her.

The dark, unexplored, unrecognised shadow side may appear as a 'spirit', as in this dream:

> I sometimes wake up in a panic when I feel as if a spirit is about to snatch me. I feel as though something is hovering over me. I wake up screaming and frighten everyone else in the house.

Eliminating the shadow

> This nightmare had stayed with me for the past ten years. I am one of three women who are possessed by ancient spirits or forces. We are shunned by everyone and eventually undergo a long and painful exorcism. When it is over the elder chieftain tells me that the other two are rid of their spirits, but mine is the most ancient, powerful and deep-seated; nothing can dislodge it. He warns me that it might rise up and take me over, and I will be powerless to prevent it.

What is this primeval force? What calls so deeply from this dreamer's core? Maybe she has become so alienated from the wise woman, that archetypal part of all of us, that her dreams call her to reconnect.

> It's a nasty dream. There is a massive hall and I'm swimming with friends. Up a winding staircase, lawn and castle and through windows are terrible things — black birds, nuns being cut up. I ran away screaming. Ran away from the yard, which had changed into my father's work yard. Now I'm afraid of going to castles.

Although the dream was two years old, Bernadette was still afraid. What was the relationship with her father? This change holds some significance for the dreamer. In his yard, in his territory, she is safe. Yet all around her is violence and confusion. She is outside looking in and she escapes, but nobody else seems to see the danger or help her out. What of the nun? Is this an aspect of her religious views or ideas about celibacy? Or could it be a word play on 'none'? There are black birds, and nuns used to wear black habits, so what does this colour mean to Bernadette?

Anxiety is a recurrent theme in dreams. It typically reveals itself in dreams of teeth falling out, being in a public place with no clothes on, being unable to find toilets and of being late. Then there are the ones we looked at earlier: being chased, attacked and hurt in some way. Houses are a common dream image and reveal much about our anxieties and shadow side.

Survey your dream houses

Houses in dreams are far from safe. They are broken into, burnt down or under siege. If you have such a dream, it may indicate that you feel insecure about your home. Are you scared you will be broken into? If so, you can do something practical to improve the situation. If, on the other hand, you aren't worried about your house, then try viewing the house as yourself, the dreamer. As Deirdre reveals:

> Sometimes I dream that I am at home and someone is trying to break in. I pick up the telephone to dial for help, but however many times I dial the number, it won't connect.

Many women dream about their house being broken into. Ciara, whose dream recurred over many months, thought it came from anxiety about being burgled but, having repeatedly checked the house to make sure it was secure, she found that the dream did not go away. Then she realised that she felt invaded:

> It suddenly dawned on me that I felt everyone was getting to me all the time. If it wasn't one person who was coming round to tell me their troubles, it would be the boss getting me to do more and more research in my own time. I felt as if the whole of my life was taken over by other people. When I recognised this, after that dream had been going on for ages, I made some changes. Now, no more dreams of being broken into!

If the dreamer is trapped inside a house, it is useful to consider whether this reflects a sense of being trapped in everyday life, that there is 'no way out'.

Ruth similarly dreamt of a house at a stressful point in her life:

> I was in a Japanese-style room with paper walls. I had to get out but couldn't get through the paper. Then two men appeared and showed me the way to the door. This dream was probably reflecting the unhappy state of my marriage at the time.

Ruth's points of escape have not been blocked. She is aided by two men who show her the route. The setting is very specific. Does Ruth know a place like this? Has she been to Japan, or has someone told her of such a room? An important point in this dream is that the walls are paper; they can be ripped or stepped through, but for some reason Ruth doesn't want to go through that paper. Does the paper equal the 'bit of paper', as the marriage licence is often called? Does she not want to destroy that? In any event, Ruth and her husband managed to resolve their problems after much reasonable discussion over ritual cups of tea — just as in a Japanese tea ceremony.

Once 19-year-old Laura told me about her childhood, the symbolism in her dream became easy to understand, although initially its meaning was not obvious to either of us:

> I have been having this dream for as long as I can remember. I am in a room which has no doors or windows and it has plain walls. In the middle is a table and chair where I am sitting. Above me is a light that has no shade and is very bright. While I am sitting there the walls and ceiling start to close in on me. When they get to a foot away from me, I wake up, crying.

There is no sight of the outside world from this windowless, doorless, unadorned room. There is only the unremitting glare of the light, terrorising the isolated girl. Finally the harsh world closes in on her. The setting is typical of an interrogation. As a child she was 'pressed' to keep away from other children. She exosted in a 'closed-off' world.

Imprisonment comes in many forms. It can be physical or psychological.

The sense of threat crops up in different guises in our dreams. In this, the 'Dark Black Cloud' dream, Georgina has a sense of overwhelming fear:

> I dreamt I looked out of my kitchen window, and outside was the darkest black cloud I have ever seen. I went upstairs to tell my husband, and as I was about to warn him of the approaching storm, something shot out of the sky and landed in our swimming pool, which sent a sheet of water over the entire garden. Then there was the most deafening noise, and the entire house started to shake and sway. I knew that I was going to have to rescue my son who was only a toddler (in fact he's 21 next week), but I also knew that if I didn't get out of the house quickly I would be buried under a pile of debris. I was so immobilised by indecision and fear that my head began to swim and I felt myself fainting. At this point I woke up, and I was really frightened.

Understandably shaken by the dream, Georgina realised she needed to look at the 'foundation' of her relationships, which appears to be under attack. Certainly, this 'black cloud' is bigger than anything encountered so far. She could look back to the time when her son was a small child to see if the roots lie there. This dream of being 'overwhelmed' is characteristic of people who have experienced trauma. The dream disguises the original event, but leaves the feeling of tremendous threat.

Houses on fire

If you dream about houses that are on fire, check to see if there are any fire hazards in your own house. Kathy had several dreams about a fire at her home and worried her mother to such an extent that she was eventually persuaded to have the electric wiring looked at. Some wires under the floor were faulty, and the electrician told them the house could have gone up in flames at any time.

If there are no physical reasons for anxiety about fire, consider what the symbol fire might mean. Is something getting too hot to handle so that it threatens to engulf you? Are you afraid that you may get burnt by playing with fire? For Jean, fire in her dream childhood house was welcomed. Quite often dream settings are places from the past, and the events of that time and place hold a key to the dream meaning:

> I dream that I am in my childhood home. The house is very untidy and dirty and I don't know where to start to clean up. A fire starts and everything is burnt. I'm filled with relief for the house is purified.

The strains of the last 13 months were showing in Jean's dream. Her elderly mother, senile and partly paralysed, had been staying at Jean's house, and Jean admitted death would be a release for both of them. She associated the fire in the dream with the act of cremation, a purifying of the no-longer functioning body. Through her dream Jean accepted that she was under a great deal of pressure.

Doors

Doors in dreams are like doors in waking life — they can act as barriers or entrances. Sometimes the dreamer has control over these doors, whereas in other instances they are beyond her control. Melissa had a dream of the latter sort:

> I am trying to lock a door that won't lock. However much I turn the key to lock it, it makes no difference; whenever I turn the handle, the door will still open. I try to phone for help but the phone is broken.

In dreams where doors figure prominently, try to work out why they won't close, or lock or open. Is there something you feel you cannot close off, or lock away or be open to? And if, like Melissa, you can't get through on the phone because it is damaged, ask yourself in what circumstances you have difficulty communicating. Telephones and doors are both means of communication so, if they don't work in your dreams, ask yourself why. Glenda was not able to protect herself far from it, she was 'compelled' to let danger in:

> I walk up to a door and am compelled to open it even though I know there is some unspeakable horror on the other side.

In a typical anxiety dream the object, place or person you are trying to reach recedes as you get closer. Catriona's dream is in the same style:

> I'm in a long room with a door at the end. I walk across but never seem to reach the door.

It reflects the frustration she feels about the seemingly never-ending task of studying for her articles as a solicitor. Catriona is still striving in her waking life, just as she is in the dream.

An intruder forces his way into Jennie's dream house and she finds that, however hard she tries, she cannot scream. She cannot move, nor can she quieten her breath in the darkened room as she lies waiting for whoever it is to make his way to her bedroom. She says that the intruder's motives are violent, never sexual. The daughter of a heavy-handed father, Jennie went on to marry 'a drinker and a beater', who regularly beat her up. Her dreams repeat her waking pattern: she is immobilised and dumb, just as she was when the victim of violence. Now, after a period in a refuge for battered women, she is starting anew, but she still relives her powerlessness in her dreams.

Rooms

Rooms have different functions just as people have different roles to play. In the following dreams, the descriptions of the rooms reveal varying aspects of the dreamer's world. Jung believed that the different levels of a house represent the different levels of being. It is at the deepest level that our most primitive instincts are to be found. Facing such instincts or coming close to our 'roots' can be disturbing, as Lenore found:

> This is a recurring dream. It is a large house and I know all the rooms on the ground floor. There are lots of rooms but I usually just stay in the one room. Other people don't realise that there are many rooms in the basement, one of which is circular. However, I get very frightened and never look any further ... When I say they don't realise the size of the house, I mean it is big enough to hold two families, two houses in one really ... I have had this dream on and off for about seven years, and I would say that I knew all the house and what was in every room at one point. I have explored all of the basement area, but I don't do so any more as I know I'm not going to like what I see.

It is as if the dreamer has two distinct sides, symbolised by the two 'families', which could co-exist harmoniously if only Lenore would accept it. She has explored the basement, the foundation, and she didn't like what was there. Something is so dreadful that it must remain locked away, concealed in the dark depths. She says she usually stays in the one room. Could this mean that she stays in one role, which she finds secure, rather than using all the other 'rooms' at her disposal? She has retreated to a place of safety and now, conveniently, she does not know what is in all the rooms that she once had the courage to explore. Lenore is cutting herself from her own potential by staying in her 'comfort zone'.

Many anxious room dreams reflect lonely isolation, as in Roisin's case, where she finds herself in a room where no-one remembers her: 'I am being completely ignored.' Others pose all sorts of threats. Ina found that, in her absence, her landlady had let her room to someone else. Ina was feeling overlooked and lonely at the time. In neither instance is the room a secure place. In another dream, she says:

> I am in a lift and it is going to crash straight through the ceiling. It always stops just in time, but the space I have to crawl through is very tight. I feel I will suffocate.

She avoids going through the roof, but it is still a struggle, with little 'space' for her.

Alison's dream affected her to the extent that she would not take a lift — and six floors up is a long way to walk! She told me what had happened:

> I had a dream about the lift at work but, instead of going up to the second floor from the ground floor, it went down. (In fact it can only go up from the ground.) When the doors opened there was an old oak door. It was very dark and the air was musty. I just jumped awake and I was frightened. When I awoke it was time to get up for work. I would not get in the lift that day, and the day after it was a real ordeal when I did use it. Since then I will not go in the lift on my own.

Something has disturbed Alison, which colours her waking days. Has she noticed something about the lift that makes her think it unsafe? She may not be consciously aware of this, but it might have lodged in her unconscious mind. Or does the lift symbolically take Alison to that deeper, Jungian level of instinct and intuition, collective communications? That part of her appears to be demanding recognition.

Walls and roofs

The walls and roof of a house provide essential protection. They keep out the worst of the natural elements: rain, wind, snow and hail, and the sun too. They act as a barrier. At home, they provide a private refuge from the outside world. However, sometimes the sense of security has gone and we dream of cracks in walls, ceilings falling in or some damage to the structure. Where these flaws become larger and more noticeable, the dreams warn us that we need to find a way of protecting ourselves, physically or emotionally.

Unfinished business is a facet of many dreams. In Meri's case it is symbolised by her previous home, which she keeps going back to in her dreams. The walls and roof give no protection:

> I have been having this dream for two years now. I keep going back to a flat I lived in many years ago. My furniture is still there, though water is pouring down the walls. Somehow the furniture is undamaged. The council have not been in touch with me at all, and I haven't paid rent in all these years, but nothing has been moved. The roof leaks too. I want to take down the curtains and wash them, but I don't want anyone to know I'm there.

Part of her — her mental 'furniture', if you like — has stayed attached to that flat or events that happened there. Everything has been left just as it was and, although Meri would like to wash the curtains, she is afraid of being discovered. Curtains are a way of excluding prying eyes and keeping separate the public and private worlds, and are not fixed. She can choose when to close them and when to open them.

Meri is afraid that someone will find out that she is there. Why does she need to hide? What does she fear? She could use the dream to discover what needs to be reclaimed from that time.

In this next dream the house seems to symbolise something that has regrettably been lost:

> I have a recurring dream about a bungalow that we lived in when we were first married 17 years ago. The dreams are never happy ones, though we were happy when we lived there. We sold it because I could not get a job, so we moved back to my home town and have been here for 15 years. In one dream, I went out of the bungalow for a walk, and I could not find it when I came back. In another dream, the bungalow was hidden in a wood and it was very run-down. In the last dream, both my husband and I were in the bungalow, but it was very cold and felt more like a prison than a home.

Jenny is obviously not happy with the way her life and marriage have turned out. Nothing major, it would seem, just a pervading feeling of disappointment. Her house disappears or is 'hidden and run-down'. Where is that happy woman of 17 years ago? She has lost sight of who she is and is physically frailer, not because of old age but because she feels lack of self-worth. Jenny recognised that she is 'run-down' because she feels depressed. Her marriage does not give her the same comfort and meaning that it once did, and she seems to be saying that she and her husband are imprisoned by their proximity rather than enriched by it.

Clare's house dream, like so many others, indicates unfinished business from the past:

> I am divorced with two children at school and am still friendly with my ex-husband. The other week I dreamt I

> was in a big house, and he came in and put all his belongings into the whole house and just stayed there.

Her husband can move back in at any time without consulting Clare. In the dream she is passive and exerts no power, even though he takes over the whole house by spreading his belongings everywhere. She doesn't complain; in fact, there is a sense of inevitability about it. This mirrors the situation in waking life. She still consults her ex-husband about every decision and firmly believes she can never really 'leave' him. It is as if there is a chain that binds them together, and Clare has forged it. She has given him her power; she has tacitly given him permission to control her life. Divorce or no divorce, she doesn't feel independent. He can 'move back any time'. The dream is very direct in its message, but only Clare can make the decision to live her own life.

When you dream about a house, pay attention to the atmosphere you find there. Is it warm and welcoming? Do you feel that it is well-cared for, or is it dilapidated and run-down? Are the outer, protective walls in good repair or are they falling down; indeed, is anyone pulling the walls down? Is it merely a shell? Examine the details closely; they can provide a wealth of information to help you understand your authentic self.

Gina finds her house, her self, ultimately secure. She has the power to look after herself:

> In my recurring dream someone is trying either to kidnap me or kill me. I run through the streets around my house — it's always late at night — and I get to my house just in time. I'm safe.

Falling and being late

When I run dream workshops or give talks, I am regularly asked whether if you hit the ground in a falling dream, you will die. For those of you who also wonder about this, let me reassure you that I have talked to lots of people who did hit the ground and they lived to tell me all about it! Instead of crashing into hard ground, the dreamer finds the surface becomes a soft cloud or springy moss. However, most women find these dreams distressing and unpleasant, and there are hundreds of variations on the theme: 'I dream I am falling down pits. Spinning and spinning. It's hard to breathe, as if something is pushing against my chest'; 'I am falling down a long, bottomless tunnel'; 'I am being pushed over the edge of a cliff'. In the Talmud, falling dreams were said to symbolise dishonour. For Freud, as you might anticipate, there was a sexual link. He thought that if a woman dreams of falling it signifies that she sees herself as a fallen woman.

A common underlying factor for the dreamer who has falling dreams is the impulse to give up, to let go. Maybe part of us wants the ground to open up beneath our feet! This is sometimes because of self-destructive tendencies, when we turn our anger inward. Instead of directing angry feelings outward to where they belong, we often hold on to them, and this can lead to feelings of depression. Rates of depression in women are high, and a significant factor in this is that we do not express anger but repress it.

The theme of being late is also very common. We are late for appointments, worried we will not meet deadlines, anxious that we won't be there to pick up the children from school; we just miss the train or stand gasping as the boat pulls out from the dock! Whatever the event the dream reveals the sense of frustration and being held back. The underlying note usually shows we are fearful that we will get into trouble, and someone will be angry with us. All such worries are tinted by that familiar emotion, guilt.

Clothes

In dreams our persona or personal 'image' is often represented by clothing. Clothes are suited to events and occupations, and provide a form of protection. They conceal disfigurements and emphasise attributes. Clothes allow us to express our feelings and give us something to hide behind. Many women have anxiety dreams in which clothes, or the lack of them, are the central feature. As you may recall, these anxiety dreams often begin in childhood.

Sometimes the clothes are totally unsuitable for the dreamer's situation. This is what happens to Vivien, a reluctant teacher:

> Every term, before school starts, I dream that I set off for school either naked or in totally the wrong clothes. As I walk along I realise I have time to change, and rush back, only to find I've got the wrong clothes on again. When I try to return to school, I find the roads have all changed. The familiar route is now strange; there are dead ends and wrong turnings.

Bridget, an Irish friend of mine, has struggled over many years to shake off traditions and expectations that are outdated for the life she now leads. She's changed a lot since she left the small village in Wexford to do her art course in London. However, her dream reveals that she cannot strip all the past away, for her early experiences are a second skin that is not easily peeled off:

> I am trying to cross a river, taking off my clothes in order to swim more easily, only to find further sets of clothing underneath. Thus, I never actually achieve this.

Like other dreamers, there is a strong need to 'change'. Bridget wants to change and cast off useless exteriors, but it is hard to strip the layers away. The clothes, the symbolic outer layer of early experiences, hinder and constrain her.

In Morag's dream she has no control over her 'image', no matter how often she tries to change it:

> I was wearing a bright pink dress down the road, and I was constantly going back home to change it, but I kept coming out in the same dress.

Bright colours draw attention, and Morag cannot change things. What is it in Morag that demands attention? Is it the predatory 'hunting pink' of fox hunters that she is wearing? Perhaps it is the pink traditionally associated with femininity or the famous Schiaparelli 'shocking pink'? And what is significant about the dress? This dream can help Morag discover her true 'image'; it is certainly eye-catching.

NAKED TRUTH

We need a protective outer layer to guard the sensitive psyche, and it needs to work with us rather than against us. In the following dreams, when the outer layer, the surface 'image', has gone, the dreamers feel embarrassed and exposed:

> I am losing my knickers in a public street. I pull them up only to watch in dismay as they fall again.

> At times of stress I dream of being naked as I walk along.

Dreams of nakedness can reveal a feeling of vulnerability. To be naked in a dream can mean that you are your natural self, stripped of pretence. However, many women feel bad about this and experience dream nakedness as being anxiety-provoking. As usual, the setting is important. If you find that you are unexpectedly naked in the dream street, does it mirror a fear of public exposure? Are you afraid that some hitherto hidden aspect of yourself might come into the open, that you will be 'stripped naked' for all the world to see? Of course, such dreams will have different meanings for different people and, for some, the anxiety may be tinged with pleasure.

In Nina's dream she is in her element, water, but that proves dangerous:

> I'm under water in a swimming pool, where I can breathe, and I am naked. There are a lot of men also naked. They have

> long hair and beards and all are skinny. They start mauling me.

Long-haired, bearded, skinny men hold some particular meaning for Nina. Here they are intrusive and uncaring. She is happy and totally at ease in this aquatic environment, but her tranquillity is broken. She is 'mauled', used and abused for no reason other than that she is there. Her relaxed nakedness is not safe. Perhaps she needs to 'swim' elsewhere in a place where she can be totally herself without being subject to 'mauling'.

If you regularly have dreams in which you are without clothes, try to make a note of when they occur. See if there is any pattern in the timing that could be linked to times of anxiety, overwork, lack of confidence, weight gain or problems in relationships.

Teeth

You may feel an empathic shudder as you hear of these 'teeth' dreams. Dreams of teeth are not new. The Chester Beatty papyrus, which dates from 2000 BCE, records dreams of teeth falling out and says they foretell death by the hands of one's dependants. In the Talmud, such dreams are said to mean that a member of the family will die.

> I'm walking up a never-ending staircase, and my teeth are falling out one by one. There is a woman laughing in the background. The dream is so realistic that I check my teeth on waking up.

> All my teeth dropping out or my mouth is full of loose teeth.

> I have a short dream which can occur within any other dream. I realise that my teeth are crumbling just like chalk pieces. I put my hand up to my chin, and they fall out into my hand in brownish-white flakes and crumbs. I have all my own teeth.

Having ensured that your teeth are not in danger of falling out in reality, consider what message your teeth dreams are imparting. What do teeth symbolise for you? Are you scared of 'showing your teeth', of getting angry? Are you worried about 'looking bad'? Are you concerned that something that has been part of your life for a long time is in fact becoming detached?

Frequently, dreams of losing teeth occur at times of separation from those to whom we are very close. Teeth are also important elements in how we look and how we appear to the world, hence the commercials that show pearly teeth with no hint of decay. Do our dreams of crumbling, dysfunctional teeth indicate some 'decay' of which we are unaware? Do such dreams indicate worry about 'losing your looks' or 'losing face'? Once again, you, the dreamer, hold the key to the significance of the dream.

Clarissa, however, after racking her brains, and having a dental check-up, could find no physical basis for her dream:

> My teeth are crumbling in my mouth, and the bits get bigger and bigger in my mouth until I feel as if I'm choking. I can feel them building up inside me.

Clarissa noticed that she had this dream at times of stress. The dream teeth block up her mouth, stop her communicating and almost prevent her from breathing. When Clarissa feels angry, does she bite back her words? Does the effort nearly choke her?

There is a myth that if you dream of swallowing one of your own teeth it means you want to get pregnant. As always, however, what the dream means varies from person to person, and our individual connections to the dream are central.

Ellen described her 'losing-teeth' dreams. In the first dreams only a few teeth became loose and then dropped out, but over time the dreams involve more teeth. In the last dream there was a solitary tooth left. Ellen remembered that when she was living at home, surrounded by her family, she never had these dreams. When she moved away to college, leaving many close friends behind, the dreams began. At first, she felt panic and fear and after the last few dreams she felt really low. In waking life she feels very isolated and vulnerable, most of her time being spent with her toddler, and she had little adult company. Because of her low income she doesn't go out much, apart from shopping and attending a group I was running in an inner city estate. It met one afternoon each week, but otherwise Ellen had no social contacts.

In talking about the dreams, Ellen was able to express herself in a way that she had not been able to do before. Marie spoke for the rest of the group when she burst out: 'Oh, Ellen, why didn't you say? I thought you just preferred to keep yourself to yourself. It would be really nice to see you more often.' The other women too wanted to see her outside the group. Since then Ellen's teeth dreams have not recurred.

Toilets

Searching for a toilet is a common dream theme. Toni's dreams have a physical trigger:

> They are many and varied. They include water flowing, oozing, cascading ... with this, I am trying to use a most unsuitable loo. It's too low, too public, too far, and I'm having great difficulty. Needless to say, I always have to visit the bathroom and the dream wakes me up.

As mentioned earlier, it is always best to look for the most obvious message, for dreams are not there to deceive the dreamer but to be of help. Toni's 'blocked loos' stop her from urinating but force her awake so that she does get to the toilet. The following dream is another example where there is an obvious physical trigger:

> One dream I've had many times recently is finding filthy, stained toilets and reacting to them with absolute disgust. No matter what the dream, the dirty toilet situation would arise. This dream intrigued me for ages, and then the interpretation came to me in a flash. Looking back, I find it

> hilarious to think of all the Freudian interpretations I tried for size on this dream! The culprit was my very own toilet, which had recently become stained with lime scale because of the practice in my small, self-contained flat of emptying teapots down it several times a day. I would think to myself, now I really must get this dealt with. I'd tried various solutions without luck and consciously had tried to remind myself to ask a friend how to deal with it. Obviously, I'd gone on remembering it in my sleep.

Physical need may prompt some toilet dreams, but not always. Karen's dream forms part of a series:

> I have a recurring theme of "No privacy on the lavatory". In the last of this series, we were staying in a hotel and I was sitting on the lavatory, which was part of our room. There were several people there, cleaners and so on, who I couldn't get rid of. I got up to go to another lavatory, and I realised, as I walked away, that my pants were down and my bottom was bare. I was mortified. I went to another one, and the situation was the same. Eyes were on me as I sat on the lavatory. It was terrible.

There are many taboos about urination and defecation, and many children are still told that anything to do with them is 'dirty', so sometimes we carry this feeling into adult dreams. Inhibited by the same worry about 'public exposure', Tina found that her friends provided the antidote she needed:

> Several in which I wanted to go to the lavatory, found it difficult to find one, and when I did it was so exposed and unprivate I couldn't use it. Lately, though, I had a dream where although it was exposed, I did use it surrounded by friends. I felt this was good.

In frustrating toilet dreams, the dreamer is being prevented from doing something that is natural to her because of fear of public scrutiny. Such scrutiny carries with it the possibility of public disapproval, which causes us great discomfort. Though toilet dreams usually reflect anxiety, for some women, such as Leah, they become a symbol for something more:

> In the past the typical dream would entail a lengthy hunt through some place I used to know well, but I could never find the loo. It was never where I thought it was. Eventually, however, I would find a loo, but there would be no privacy and no relief. Always when I woke up I would find I needed to go to the toilet — hence the lack of relief in the dream! But now the need has become a symbol for some other kind of elimination, because not only can the dream continue beyond the point at which I find the lavatory (or some suitable substitute), but also on waking there is no marked physical need to account for the dream.

Other dreams continue the development of the theme, so that elimination of 'waste material' has become a significant symbol for Leah to work on when she uses her dreams to get rid of emotional 'baggage' that hinders her progress.

THE DARK SHADOW OF DEATH

Dreams of the dead carry huge emotional impact. Some reflect the sense of loss and regret at opportunities not taken or a yearning to repeat them. Caroline's is a good example:

> I have nightmares about a dead friend and doing all the things we used to do, and in the dream knowing I'm running out of time and will wake up to reality.

The dream shows her coming to terms with the truth that in waking life she can no longer share the day-to-day events with her friend. Grieving is a process, and it happens in our dreams.

Dreams of death do not mean that you are about to die. What they may mean is that you are in the throes of some change in your life, and the form of death will provide extra clues. If you dream of dying, of being murdered, ask yourself in what way you feel under attack in waking life. What is threatening you? Such dreams can be 'wake-up' calls to draw your attention to self-destructive habits or relationships. Sometimes we appear to live but feel dead inside as Becky's dreams show:

> I dream of people I know, but in the dreams they appear to be dead, and then I notice them breathing, then their legs and arms twitching, and sometimes they actually get up and start talking to me and act as if they are still alive, and I'm terrified. Also, that I am dead but can see what's going on.

Charlene has the ever-present sense of threat in a whole range of places, but she senses that she 'knows' the would-be murderer:

> I have had a recurring nightmare for the past six to seven years. Someone is trying to murder me by stabbing or shooting. It occurs in differing forms — different countries, different people involved, set in dark rooms, caves or open spaces, etc. The strange thing is that I usually 'know' who the murderer is. I witness him/her committing several murders on other people beforehand, and in so doing become a prime suspect in other people's eyes for these crimes. Just before I am to be stabbed, shot or whatever, I wake up.

The fact that these nightmares started six or seven years ago is worth investigating. What happened then to set off these fears? Certainly, feeling high anxiety, fear or lack of trust can trigger such dreams:

> These are mainly about awful things happening to the people closest to me. A recent one was about a girl who was

> living with us for a while. She was passing me in the kitchen, and I thought, about to give me a hug. Just then I felt this dreadful pain in my back, gradually feeling numb. She had stabbed me in the back. I woke up still having this awful pain.

Florence has many dreams of death and dying, of people appearing dead but then coming alive again. She recognised that these death dreams occur because all her life she has been terrified of dying:

> Dead human bodies or parts of bodies appear in the dream, or I spend the dream time escaping from them, terrified in case I see them too clearly or touch them. Other people in the dream, if they appear, are often unafraid and casual, not sharing my fear.

Where the acts of violence are self-inflicted, then the dreamer needs to explore what it is that is causing such self-destructive acts:

> I dream that I am pregnant, that I am lying in air or water, which is rushing around me. Everything is cold and I am sticking knives into parts of my body.

This dreamer is 'pregnant', that is, something is trying to be born but there is no solidity, no grounding to. help with this confinement and delivery. Not only that, but she is damaging herself, attacking herself. Like people who cut themselves, who self-harm, she may be desperate to find out if she can feel, if she can let out some of the hurt and grief within. The coldness of the dream emphasises this lack of emotional warmth or support available to her. In another dream, she has been buried alive and is completely alone. Such desolate dreams urge us to seek help, to restore emotional well-being before it is too late.

> About four months after my husband died, his brother, who I'd never met and who had died years before I met my husband, came to me with a miner's lamp — to light the way.

Dreams of death or destruction often tells us we need to look at endings and beginnings. In the final chapter, 'The Eternal Venus', we will find that these dreams may be the key to understanding the mysteries of life.

Chapter 9

The Eternal Venus

Call the world, if you please, 'The Vale of Soul-making',
Then you will find out the use of the world.

John Keats

Transpersonal aspects of dreaming connect us to the river of life that is past, present and future. We step in and we are connected to all that has gone before, all that is happening now and all that will come. Dreams can play a key part in accessing this inner wisdom, and this chapter includes examples from different spiritual traditions in which dreams are seen as divinely inspired.

Dreams you never forget

Some dreams carry such an impact that they transform our way of thinking and feeling, touching the deep core of our being. This is especially the case in dreams of a spiritual nature. Nadia had a dream when she was ten years old, which was so vivid that she has never forgotten it:

> I dreamt of a voice coming from heaven. I knew in the dream it was God speaking to me. He told me to go inside the house because he was going to make rain fall. I obeyed and saw this beautiful green rain falling.
>
> Then the voice, God, told me to come out of the house and asked me to swim as the rain had made a type of swimming pool. I answered that I could not swim. He told me to just get into the water and I would swim. I did and I swam round without any effort or fear. It is impossible to explain the ecstasy I felt.

She comments:

> I believe the subconscious is the mediator and transmitter of all important and relevant information which is needed for personal spiritual growth. I believe our 'higher intelligence' to be linked to 'universal intelligence' and therein lies the answer to everything we need to know ... In dreams we can 'tune in' to our higher intelligence and thus gain insight into ourselves and our purpose in life.

Immanence is the sense or the experience of God in everything, in every action, in all our encounters, in every exchange we have. Whether this is the concept of Gaia, a higher spiritual knowledge, or however else you wish to label it, it is the sense of being connected to something more. It is ineffable, indescribable, unnameable, which is why it is so difficult to put into words — labelling just doesn't work here.

THE SPIRIT WITHIN

Is religious impulse innate? The answer from many is a resounding 'yes'. Across all cultures at all times we find a spiritual dynamic that indicates a natural tendency to find purpose, an instinct to discover, to find a pattern and a reason for existence. We are born ready to 'image' things, and these come in archetypes. In her recent book, *Spiritual Intelligence*, Danah Zohar writes of the research in neuroscience that has identified a 'God spot' in the temporal lobe of the brain.

The divine, the absolutely 'Other' as distinct from ourselves, is what human beings have always sought. In many cases this knowledge comes in an intuitive flash or in some kind of revelation, often in dreams. The founder of the Quakers, the Society of Friends, George Fox, said: 'I came to know God experientially.' One woman who filled in a questionnaire about dreams, which I used for my earlier research into women's dreams, wrote:

> I became frightened filling this in. I suddenly felt scared about how spiritual my dreams are in some ways, or at least

my response to them, and then I felt frightened about how that part of me seems only to exist in dreams, as if I'm two people. When I do remember dreams they are always powerful and vivid. The images fascinate me. I would like to go into them more than I make time for at the moment.

Dream guides

Modern shamanic teaching comes from Siberia, via native North American peoples. Their spiritual tradition is based on the interconnectedness of all nature and all human beings. The teaching of oneness is known as the Great Mystery, and dreams play a vital role in the process of understanding the meanings of the Great Mystery. The time of dreams is seen as a sacred way to experience and connect to the web of life. It may involve out-of-body dreams in which alternative realities or parallel universes are explored. In particular, healing dreams, or medicine dreams as they are sometimes called, bring information about the future. These rare dreams are particularly treasured and are cautiously shared with great respect.

> I had a recent dream where a female in ivory satin was leaving me and we hugged, then a cheeky, lively young male arrived in a wagon — I was sure this was one guide leaving as her job was complete. At that time my perceptions of life altered. It was time for my spirituality to be 'earthed'. I now see earth and spirit together, not separate as I used to; heaven being a place to go after death — I now realise heaven is 'in the mind' now.

Perhaps you too will find this dimension in your dream journal. In his book *Spiritual Healing in a Scientific Age*, Robert Peel writes of the divinity we each share. He links it to Christian tradition, but it applies to many other spiritual groups:

> Jesus said that he came from 'the kingdom of heaven' and said that this kingdom of God is 'with you' (Luke 17:21). So

each of us has God and heaven within us and we are all made in his image.

Intuitive dreaming

Intuition — defined as 'immediate unreasoned perception', a hunch, a feeling, a knowingness, a flash of insight — is characteristically associated with women and dreams. Dreams are a reliable source of intuitive inspiration. By sifting through the layers of meaning and by recording them you may find abilities you would reject in waking life. Intuitively we may need help, and our dreams respond by giving us a guide. Guides tutor us in skills and beliefs and protect us.

A guide, a Jungian archetype, a metaphorical figure, repeats some aspect of your unconscious mind or higher conscious mind. Some call this our soul level or higher mind. We visit this in dreams or trance states. In her book, *Trusting Your Intuition*, Sylvia Claire says: 'My own childhood guide for many years was a wonderful native American healer who taught me to cope with fear through my dreams. Just before I went to sleep he would arrive and support me in conquering my fear of darkness and night' (p149). Perhaps you too are inspired to face your fears and invite a guide to come into your dreamtime.

The soul's journey

In *I Fly Out With Bright Feathers* Allegra Taylor wrote of a dream she had as she set off on her world-wide exploration of women's spirituality. It was a numinous dream in which she found herself transformed into giant condor with a six-foot wing span. In this infinite space, above the peaks of mountains, like a 'spiny dragon's back', she eventually sought a place to rest. Like other mythic voyagers, she knew in her dream that she had a task to perform, but didn't know what it was. In the next part of the dream she falls asleep and is carried along by the thermals. In letting go of her fear and trusting she will know the task when it is put in front of her, she soars in the spheres. When she awoke from this vivid dream, Allegra checked to see if she had feathers on her arms — the symbolism was so clear she knew she was right on target in her quest.

Respect for the soul's journey toward the centre of oneself is what Jung calls the 'Self', and what Vera van der Heydt called in her book *Prospects for the Soul*, 'the vessel into which God's grace might pour.' The way we do that, she said, 'is nobody's concern but our own, and the only thing that matters is to go on looking until we catch a glimpse of where the treasure is'.

Whether we reach it or not is uncertain; it seems as if the search is more important than the goal:

> My mother-in-law usually crops up to block my progress. For example, I was rising very rapidly up through countless floors and levels of a mansion till I came to the loft, where Kay, my mother-in-law, lived, and I was angry with her because she was keeping me from rising higher. On an esoteric level she is my block, I can't develop spiritually till I learn to accept her for what she is.

Many transcendent elements in dreams involve water, which in some ways washes away old ways of life. It purifies and cleanses. Sometimes, to emphasise this, the water is in a special place, such as a temple, as it is in Laylah's dream:

> Went through a stage of having dreams of water and wells. One well was square and white-washed, and had steps leading down to it. I started to descend towards the very clear, pure light water and was told an alcove a little way down was a type of temple. I wasn't allowed to descend to it although I could stand a step or two above and look into it.

Laylah isn't ready for full immersion yet, but the destination is clear. Notice how she also has a guide who advises her. Soon after she had another dream:

> There were two of us, male and female, searching for a way through a maze. We went round in circles and ended up back where we had started. Another man met us and said, 'I've shown you the way once and look what you've done. Try again,' and pointed out the way again. We found ourselves at the bottom of a well shaft, and were told to smell the smells of things one wouldn't expect to have smells. 'Smell the smell of the sight of beauty.' 'Smell the smell of the sound of...' 'Smell the smell of the fear of...' The man was climbing ahead of me, and suddenly I reached a kind of barrier and couldn't get through, then suddenly I was through and the dream faded out.

Here she is being introduced to a completely new way of experiencing her senses and, once again, the guide is there. In this dream, she has gone through a barrier, which indicates she has progressed to another level in her journey. Anna also has a guide:

> My dreams are always very clear and vivid. They normally involve a figure who tends to lead me, acting as a guide. This figure takes on many forms. I have a guide through stress, sometimes they appear as my husband, my father, and sometimes as a faceless figure, but I am always secure.'

93-year-old Emily often dreams of her son, who lives in Australia:

> He often comes to me to give me comfort. I believe dreams can be an answer to prayer when I have been worried.

Connections to the Eternal

> So, if I dream I have you, I have you,
> for, all our joys are but fantastical.
>
> *John Donne*, Elegies (1600)

Dreams of people who have died often come to comfort and help the dreamer who meets them once again in sleep. Pat's dreams have a healing quality:

> As the youngest child, I was particularly close to my mother and had a very good relationship with her. Unfortunately, she developed Alzheimer's and died a slow, painful death. She has visited me on several occasions in my dreams, always travelling; once sitting in the back of a hearse in a beautiful dress, smiling and waving to me, and another time sitting opposite to me in a train compartment, handing me a bunch of apricot gladioli. The lunchtime of the next day, passing through M&S, there in a bucket were bunches of apricot gladioli. It felt like a statement from her that she was still with me. I find I dream about her when I am having a tough time, and that she is always around, and that is comforting. Some people will say this is all tosh and that it can be explained scientifically. Be that as it may. All I know is that it helps me.

Similar dreams help Willa:

> I sometimes dream of my dead father and husband. They always look well and do not refer to their illness. It goes unsaid as if nothing has happened, and the dreams are usually quite mundane. When I wake up I do feel, and perhaps hope, that they really have been in contact with me.

There are large areas of the brain that are like uncharted territory. We know they are there but we don't know exactly what happens there. In years to come, no doubt, the nature of these dreams and others that seem too far-fetched for some to believe, will be charted. A.H. Maslow, the American psychologist, says in his book *Religions, Values and Peak Experiences*: 'The very beginning, the intrinsic core, the essence ... of every known high religion has been the private, lonely, personal illumination, revelation or ecstasy of some acutely sensitive prophet or seer' (p.19). Often such revelations come in dreams. These 'peak experiences' or 'transcendent experiences', Maslow argues, are natural human experiences, not supernatural. Usually the prophets/seers have these experiences when they were alone, either in meditation or in dreams.

After her husband's death, Anna was devastated and found it impossible to come to terms with the fact that she would never see him again. One night she had this dream:

> I stood in a beautiful garden, long aisles of multi-coloured roses in full bloom, grand oak trees bordering the garden. The sky was a deep azure blue, no clouds and not even a breath of wind to stir the roses. I heard someone call my name. I turned and saw a figure beside me. I could not make out their face, but I knew it was my husband. He took my hand in his, and we walked together through the garden. We came to a gate in a wall at the end of the garden, he let go of my hand and stood before me. 'Will you come with me?', he asked. I did not answer, but I followed him.
>
> I was standing in a graveyard surrounded by headstones that had either fallen over and shattered or were surrounded by thick weeds. My husband was to the side of me. He took my hand and led me through the graveyard to a headstone that was clear of weeds. I stood before the stone, which had my husband's name on it. As I looked at the stone, moss began to cover it at an alarming rate, the headstone cracked and split in two. 'Come with me?' Again I did not speak.
>
> I was standing on a cliff's edge, the sea beating against the rocks at the bottom, clouds swirling like a mist just before me. My husband stood before me, amongst the mist, his arms reaching out to me. Again he asked me to go with him. I took a step towards him and then stopped. I shook my head, he smiled at me and then faded.

> I awoke at this point and then wrote the dream down. I had been feeling guilty about finding someone else, but after I wrote the dream down I thought about what it might mean. I felt that the beginning of the dream was the life I shared with my husband, good memories and the love that we shared. The second stage was loss, realising that he was gone. My husband was not buried and so had no headstone, but this obviously symbolises death. The third stage is the acceptance that I must let him go, and that I should live my life.

Dreams incorporate all the senses, and these can act as the trigger to connect to someone who has died. Pia told me that her dreams are filled with scents: 'I know when my dad comes because I can smell tobacco.

THE THIN VEIL

> Dreams come true, without that possibility, nature would not incite us to have them.
>
> *John Updike*

The veil between the seen and the unseen may be very thin at certain points, especially during life crises, mental stress and times of great upheaval. When the Tlingits, an Innuit tribe, are close to death, they give signs to each other so they will be recognised when they reincarnate. There is a great emphasis on dreams, especially those of children and pregnant women, as having prophetic powers.

Calpurnia, Caesar's wife, predicted her husband's assassination after she had a dream in which she was holding her dead husband's body in her arms. She warned him, and he tried to alter his fateful appointment but was persuaded against it by his murderer. There are many, many examples of prophetic or warning dreams that people have told me about, and such dreams have been recorded throughout history. Keeping a dream journal helps to let you know if you have predictive or telepathic dreams. Some involve 'out-of-body experiences' or astral travel, and some dream settings remind us of places we have never seen and people we have never met.

> Some of my dreams are like a mystical experience. Many times I feel I'm leaving my body and feel free and light in this type of dream. I meet people I've never met before and find myself in places I've never seen, although they frequently feel familiar. In this sort of dream I can see future or past events.

Where we have a close relationship, bonded by love or blood, communication may take place in extraordinary ways. Mary told me about what happened to her:

> Last year, when I was on a camping holiday in Portugal, I had a horrible dream that as I walked down a street someone collided right into me and I was left lying on the street, unable to get up and just twitching there. It was an awful sensation. I tried to put it down to the wine I'd drunk the night before ... Two weeks later, when I arrived at the airport, a friend was there to meet me, and told me that my mother had had a stroke while I had been away. I have always felt that the dream was some kind of acting out of her stroke, a way of communicating when I was travelling around with no way for people to get in touch with me.

Highly attuned nervous systems that enable people to pick up information that others miss can be see in children before it is 'educated out'. Children often have an imaginary friend whom they can see and hear and who is as important to them as 'real' friends:

> I have had a similar dream all my life, and I believe I retain a memory of my birth. It was a difficult birth, so my mother says, and I was eventually delivered by Caesarean. I am an only child, so dreams, daydreams and imaginary friends are probably more important to me than to a child from a large family. My family has always seen dreams as important. It seems to be a trait inherited through my father. He dreams of places and finds they exist. My paternal grandmother dreamt several times of places where my grandfather was in great danger during the First War. Perhaps a kind of telepathy is involved, for when he came home she was able to describe them to him with great accuracy. I sometimes dream the same dream at the same time as my eldest son.

Sometimes such phenomena can be afflicting, the antennae being too attuned to the world so that there is no respite.

> This was a terrible nightmare. About 12 years ago in August I awoke absolutely horrified because something ghastly had happened to our two grandchildren. It was so dreadful that I could not even tell my husband, and I repressed it, so except for the feeling I do not know what I dreamt. In September the police came and told us that our daughter-in-law had killed the children and tried to commit suicide. This happened 4–6 weeks after the dream. She had post-natal depression, but we knew nothing about this, six months after the second child was born. I often wonder why such a dream should occur, and if I had taken notice of it could I have prevented such a thing?

Tara had a dream when she was 21:

> I dreamt of my boyfriend being stabbed. I woke up suddenly, it was 12.30. I thought of calling him, I was so afraid. I felt this dream so strongly, but still I decided to wait

> until the morning. When I rang him in the morning, he told me his brother had been stabbed at 12.00 by some guys who were trying to steal his money.

Many people are frightened when they have this kind of dream. It defies rational explanation, yet such dreams are more common than people realise. Perhaps, like Tara, you have some level of awareness that can be tuned into, like a highly sensitive antenna that can pick up signals others are deaf to. The thin veil lets information in which others cannot receive.

Some dreams that come through the veil are useful as preparation for events to come. Subliminal information is transmitted to our brains all day long but may only become apparent through dreams:

> I had one about my dad getting ill, and he was in hospital dying, but he recovered. A few months later my dad found out he had TB and pleurisy. This dream was helpful because it prepared me, and when he told us I wasn't as shocked and I knew he was going to recover.

> I had a dream in which I was comforting my cousin. Her father died two days later. I was totally unaware of his health problems before he died.

Neither of these dreamers had waking thoughts about the events that happened.

Final judgement

Part of living is to recognise that life is impermanent. Once we accept that we are not immortal, we wonder about death and what comes after. Our dreams wrestle with this ultimate question. The content ranges from the glorious to the horrendous:

> I remember one where I died and went to heaven. It was a

> marvellous place filled with beautiful angels. Lots of gold flashing.
>
> I am dropped by a taxi in my town centre at the dead of night. I look for a bus. Everything is shut up. There are no buses, no people, everywhere is deserted, not even cars going by. An empty chip bag blows along in the wind. The black sky darkens further and there is a clap of thunder. In this dream I experienced a feeling of such utter loneliness and abandonment. There was a feeling of it being the final judgement. Such feelings I wish never to feel, ever again.
>
> I had a particularly unusual dream: I was standing in the drive at the front of my house when in the midst of a dream I saw a dark cloud, and from that cloud reached forth the hand of God straight down towards me from heaven, forefinger outstretched. And I reached up in similar fashion to touch the hand of God, because I was keen to please Him. At my feet He flung a harness and I, not knowing what to do with it, for want of somewhere better, placed it under a fir tree.

This dream last reminded me of the painting of Adam in the Sistine Chapel, where God reaches from heaven to spark life into the recumbent man. There is the element of creation here. The fir tree extends this theme. It was used by the Druids to represent the rebirth of the sun and, as all evergreens, it symbolises immortality, because it keeps on going when other trees seem to have 'died' in winter.

DEATH OR NEVER-ENDING LIFE?

Dreams in which the dreamer dies do not predict instant death, rather they represent the end of part of the dreamer's life. After a divorce, for instance, women often dream that someone has died, frequently themselves. These dreams are metaphors that express that our feeling for someone, or someone's feelings for us, have ended and that phase of our life is over.

Angie has had a number of dreams that indicated future events. She said: 'The most significant one was of death.' When she woke up she was feeling very disturbed and cried for hours. When she thought about her dream she realised that it wasn't about a physical death but about the breaking down of her 'old' self. That day she made new friends and began 'a new cycle of existence'.

> I had some very vivid dreams when I was 15 about a friend who had died in a car crash earlier that year. In the dreams she was alive but was hiding from everyone. I wanted to tell her mum, but she told me not to. It felt so real I kept expecting to see her, even though I knew I wouldn't. In other instances, we reunite with people who have already died.

Death in all major religions involved meeting the gods or God. In fact, Greek doctors, influenced by Hippocrates, believed it was not ethical to treat a dying patient because to do that was to fly in the face of the gods. There would be revenge, fateful hubris, if they set themselves up against the divine. Plato, known as the father of Western philosophy, wrote:

> The cure of the part should not be attempted without treatment of the whole ... for this is the greatest error of our day in the treatment of the human body that physicians first separate the soul from the body.

When we tend our dreams we tend the world

Tend the dream, tend the world. Women are using dreams as part of an ecological approach to looking after the planet. Dreams of nuclear wars, hurricanes, floods and tidal waves tell us of concerns we have for our world as well as ourselves.

> One dream I had helped me in as much that however bad things seem to be, everything will turn out all right in the end. In this dream I was walking along a dark lane. Trees on either side had large branches, which hid the sky and no light was getting through. Besides the trees there was a high stone wall running on either side as far as the eye could see, and the feeling of gloom was everywhere. Suddenly I came to a wooden door in this wall. I opened it, and went through into a glorious garden, full of colour, the sun was shining and the sky was blue, there was wonderful music coming from somewhere, and I felt gloriously happy and at peace with life.

Dreaming is the medium through which the deeper self communicates with the conscious bodily self, using images and feelings that are languages of the sensory body. Our material life is merely the tip of the iceberg, the rest is unseen. These dreams also connect us with the earth, Mother Earth, which is under such threat at the present time.

Women are dreaming about environmental issues. These dreams release tensions about what is happening to our planet, as Suzette's dream reveals:

> A few months ago I dreamt that I was in a house with a lot of people around me, and suddenly rivers of fire started to surround us. We escaped outside, but still it was the same. I felt that a volcano had erupted. I then dreamt I was on some kind of surface and flying into the sky, over the red-hot streams of fire that had covered the whole land. I looked down and could see people screaming and running away.

She had been watching a television documentary on climate change and felt that her dream images captured her concerns about the survival of the planet.

Concern about our world starts in childhood for some

women. Alice had two recurring dreams as a child. In the first the 'heat' is turned on Alice and she feels in danger. In the other, disaster is imminent:

> In one dream the furnace in my family's basement in our home came alive and chased me around the house. I couldn't run because my legs were like rubber. I wasn't caught, but I can distinctly remember the feeling of panic. My other recurring childhood dream was about a world disaster, and my neighbourhood being in chaos and feeling helpless.

How far do such dreams reflect generalised anxiety about the natural world? Such dreams can tell us we need to actively protect Mother Earth. Other dreams reflect early awareness of the effect of climate change. Alice told me:

> Several years ago I dreamt that I was in the middle of a war. I had my younger brother with me — he must have been around six years old. He and I were near a public lavatory. The building was enclosed by a cyclone fence, so we could see what was going on through the fence. I remember feeling frantic and wanting to find a place to hide with my brother. Both of us ran inside the public lavatory. There was stainless steel receptacle on the wall. I threw my brother inside the receptacle then climbed inside with him. I remember feeling as if we were in danger.

Emotions are reason's ally, not its enemy. In our dreams the emotions of fear and loss can help our logical side. Hand in hand, feeling and thought can help us in this journey that is life and aid us in our attempts to tend the world.

Dreams of the dead carry huge emotional impact. Some reflect the sense of loss and regret at opportunities not taken or a yearning to repeat them. Caroline's is a good example:

> I have nightmares about a dead friend and doing all the things we used to do, and in the dream knowing I'm running out of time and will wake up to reality.

Dreams for a mythic journey

As shown in the ideas of and research of Joseph Campbell, the tale of this journey is told in all cultures — by the Buddha, Moses, Jesus, Mohammed. It is about the vision quest for spiritual enlightenment. The quest may involve a long dark night of the soul where we open ourselves to accusations of being crazy or selfish, and, because we are afraid of being different from others we turn our backs on the quest and stay in our comfortable ruts. It requires us to wander and wait through suffering, and it always lasts longer than we want it to. This is a spiritual apprenticeship in which we face our fears and find our wisdom.

Four kinds of dreams are needed for a mythic journey:

- Calling
- Quest
- Illumination
- Return.

The calling may come at any time, with a nagging sense that we want something else, with a feeling of emptiness. In fairy tales the calling comes when the plague hits the land or a barrenness descends or a dragon seeks sacrificial victims in the form of young women. We feel 'in the dark' but that is all part of the process. We need to be in a dark place in order to grow:

> I have one that occurs frequently: the sun sets over the sea, I am alone on the beach. To my left is a tree, bare of leaves, to my right is an ancient ruin, I think from the Roman era. Something is calling out to me, but I can never hear or reach whoever is there. (Anna)

In calling dreams you may meet a benefactor who tenders advice, suggests you make a journey or offers instruction. There may be dreams in which you are stuck or going round and round in circles. There may be abduction dreams where you are pulled along by a force beyond your control. In other dreams you may be in a ship without a captain or travelling in a moving car which has no driver, or having to escape.

> I have had dreams involving fleeing from water which threatened to engulf me. This theme reoccurred often at a time of emotional crisis.

During the quest part of the journey, before we find illumination or enlightenment, there are several stages. These include dreams of murder and betrayal of values peopled by enemies in which there is an abject fear of annihilation. There are dreams of despair and frustration, anxiety about whether to change or not, and a sense of time running out. In our dreams we ask ourselves 'will I make it?'

Gradually dreams may reflect the fact that changes are afoot. They are bizarre and novel. Change is no longer threatening but surprising. We might have strange, alien images, for instance, you bite into an apple and it changes into heart, or an animal that is growing so fast it seems like a speeded-up film. Then we have the guides and mentors who come with their words of wisdom to help us to truly experience the change we have been questing for. To find the philosopher's stone, the holy grail, we need to look with our eyes and see with our heart.

> A few months ago I dreamt I was overlooking a lake which people in long robes were walking into. At first I was troubled that they were killing themselves, and then I realised it was some form of baptism. I heard a movement behind me and I turned to see an Indian man (small with such a kind face). I was so pleased to see him, and we hugged each other as old friends. Then a young Indian girl took me

into a room and said (I feel telepathically) that "they" wanted me to stay with them, and I so wanted to. Then a man appeared. He looked at me with cold eyes, and I knew I would leave with him reluctantly.

The three people in the dream are not familiar to me, but I felt it was showing me what is going on in my life at present and that I have to break a pattern of pleasing others at my own expense. It was showing me, I think, what deep within I know, that people are waiting for me when I find the courage to say no to others. (Norma)

When illumination comes, we see it in dreams where darkness becomes light and what was puzzling becomes plain to us at last. In Taoism, the Far Eastern philosophy, the importance of darkness and light is central. Tao means 'the way of nature', and it is natural to experience the dark as well as the light, despair as well as joy.

Change is no longer threatening but embraced, and is life-enhancing. Then we return once more to where we set off from. We integrate what we have learned on our journey to embody the new way we've discovered to be. This cyclical, mythic journey is necessary for us to discover the creative, spiritual beings we truly are.

This dream includes many aspects of the mythic journey:

The fear of water dreams seemed extremely significant. They seemed to help me keep my bearings, by putting an image on the fear and turbulence. Sometimes I would also dream that I was enjoying riding on the waters, playing with the water — very reassuring. I once dreamt of a horrifying encounter with hideous, decaying, skeletal corpses, wearing cloaks. When I related this to a wise friend, I was advised, 'next time, turn and embrace these spectres'. There was no next time, and there has never been a dream of that nature since. My psyche now knows how to cope, as I accepted the principle that it is necessary to embrace what one fears.

Sophia accepts that fears are the calling cards that move us towards insight.

Our dreams are signposts on our eternal quest, as Deborah concluded:

> The significant dreams sometimes throw a new light on to something important. Either the symbolism is so loaded and has such emotional power that I know it is worth pondering and trying to understand what it is saying; or the dream acts out, or causes me to act out, situations that are informative. I have had dreams when I acted with great calmness and presence in certain circumstances. The feeling stays with me for a while, as if my psyche is subtly changed by it. Either way, I have learned something and something rich, too much to articulate clearly.

Before you move off to travel your personal mythic journey using your dreams, there is one Venus we have not yet met. She is the well-rounded figurine of the Venus of Wallendorf, one of the oldest carved stone statues still in existence. She is the goddess as a life force, and represents a cosmology that sees our relationship with the earth and all living things as one breathing organism. She stands for the way in which we are all connected by the web of life. In our dreams we weave the web, we repair it and we nurture both ourselves and all life. Cherish you dreams as you cherish yourself.

References

Allende, Isabel, 'The *Guardian* Interview', *The Guardian*, 5 February 2000

Artemidorus, *The Interpretation of Dreams, Oneirocritica*, trans. Robert J. White, Noyes Press, Park Ridge, N.J., 1975

Balon, R., 'Bupropion and nightmares' (letter), *American Journal of Psychiatry*, 153 (4), April 1996, 579–80

Benedek, Thérèse and Rubinstein, Boris, 'The Correlations bewteen ovarian activity and psychodynamic processes', in *Pyschosomatic Medicine*, vol 1, no. 2, April 1939

Bolander, Donald, *The New Webster's Dictionary of Quotations and Famous Phrases*, 1987 (John Updike)

Boss, Medard, *The Analysis of Dreams*, Rider, London, 1957

Bulkeley, Kelly, *Spiritual Dreaming: A Cross-cultural and Historical Journey*, Paulist Press, N.J., 1962

Caine, Marti, *A Coward's Chronicle*, Century, London, 1990

Campbell, J., *Myths to Live By*, Bantam Books, New York, USA, 1972

Candace, B., Pert, *Molecules of Emotion*, Simon & Schuster, UK Ltd, 1997

Cheek, D.B., 'The significance of dreams in initiating premature labour', *American Journal of Clinical Hypnosis*, 12 (1), 1969, 5–15

Circot, J.E., *A Dictionary of Symbols*, trans. Jack Sage, Routledge & Kegan Paul, London, 1962

Clarke, Sylvia, *Trusting Your Intuition*, Oxford, Pathways, 1999

Cohen, D., 'Sex role orientation and dream recall', *Journal of Abnormal Psychology*, 82, 1973, 246–52

Craighead, Meinrad, *The Mother's Songs: Images of God the Mother*, Paulist Press, USA, 1982

Delaney, Gayle, *In Your Dreams*, HarperCollins, San Francisco, 1997

de Martino, M.F., 'Sex differences in the dreams of Southern college students', *Journal of Clinical Psychology*, 9, 1953

Douvan, Elizabeth, 'Sex differences in adolescent character processes', in *Readings of the Psychology of Women*, ed. Judith M. Bardwick, Harper & Row, New York, 1972

Estes, Clarissa, Pinkola, *Women Who Run With the Wolves*, Rider, London, 1992

Faraday, Ann, *The Dream Game*, Harper & Row, New York, 1972

Garfield, P., *Creative Dreaming*, New York, NY, Ballantine, 1994

Garland, Caroline, *Understanding Trauma*, Gerald Duckworth + Co. Ltd, UK, 1998

Gehry, Frank, 'Bilbao architect puts his stamp on Dundee — for free!', article by Fred Bridland, *The Independent on Sunday*, 23 July 2000

Guiley, Rosemary Ellen, *Dreamwork for the Soul*, Berkley Books, New York, NY, 1998

Hall, C. and Domhoff, B., 'A ubiquitous sex difference in dreams', *Journal of Abnormal and Social Psychology*, 66, 9173

Hall, Nor, *The Moon and the Virgin*, The Women's Press, London, 1980

Hartman, E.H., *The Biology of Dreaming*, Charles Thomas, Boston 1967

Hartmann, Ernest, *Dreams and Nightmares: The New Theory on the Origin and Meaning of Dreams*, Plenum, New York, 1998

Havelock, Ellis, *Studies in the Psychology of Sex*, Random House, New York, 1942

Hillman, James, *The Dream and the Underworld*, Harper & Row, Philadelphia, 1979

Hughes, J. Donald, 'Dream interpretations in ancient civilisations', *Dreaming*, 10 (1), 2000

Hyman, S., 'Conception and dream material during psycho-analysis', *Journal of Contemporary Psychotherapy*, 10, 1979, 136–44

Jenks, Kathleen, Pacificia Graduate Institute Programme, 2000–2001, p17

Jones, Celia, 'An exploratory study on women's manifest dreams during first pregnancy', PhD thesis, Columbia University, 1978

Jung, C.J., *Man and His Symbols*, Aldus Books Ltd, London, 1964

Kabat-Zinn, Jon, *Full Catastrophe Living: How to Cope with Stress, Pain and Illness Using Mindfulness Meditation*, Piatkus, London, 1996

Karpman, Steven B., 'Fairy tales and script drama analysis', *Transactional Bulletin*, 7 (2), April 1968, 39–48

Kilroe, Patricia A., 'The dream pun: what is a play on words without words?', *Dreaming*, 10 (4), 2000

Kinsey, A. *et al.*, *Sexual Behaviour in the Human Female*, W.B. Saunders, New York, 1953

Koestler, Arthur, quoted in Annie Wilson, *The Wise Virgin: The Missing Link Between Men and Women*, Turnstone Books, London, 1979

Lunnen, Mary, *Flying In The Face of Fear: Surviving Cervical Cancer*, Hypatia Trust, Newmill, U.K., 1998

McCormack, Elizabeth, Wilde, *Living on the Edge*, Element Books, Shaftesbury, Dorset, 1997

Mallon, Brenda, *Women Dreaming*, Fontana, London, 1987

—— *Children Dreaming*, Penguin, Harmondsworth, 1989

—— *Creative Visualization with Colour*, Element, Dorset, 1999

—— *An Illustrated Guide To Dreams*, David & Charles, London, 2000

—— *Dreams, Counselling and Healing*, Gill & Macmillan, Dublin, 2000

Malone, C., Farthing, L. and Marce, L. (eds.), *The Memory Birds: Survivors of Sexual Abuse*, Virago, London, 1996

Mankowitz, Ann, *Change of Life: A Psychological Study of Dreams and the Menopause*, Inner City Books, Canada, 1984

Maslow, A.H., *Religions, Values and Peak Experiences*, Viking Penguin, Harmondsworth, 1976

Masson, J.M., *The Assault on the Truth: Freud's Suppression of the Seduction Theory*, Faber, London, 1984

Myss, Caroline, *Anatomy of Spirit*, Bantam Books, London, 1997

Oates, Joyce Carol, 'This one could run and run', *The Guardian*, 22 July 1999

O'Brien, Edna, 'Me and my psyche', *The Weekend Guardian*, 11–12 March 1989

Peel, Robert, *Spiritual Healing in a Scientific Age*, Harper & Row, San Francisco, 1987

Phillips, A. and Rakusen, J. (eds.), *Boston Women's Health Book Collective: Our Bodies, Ourselves*, Penguin, Harmondsworth, 1979

Phillips, Helen, 'Cycling in your sleep', *New Scientist*, 25 September 1999

Pomeroy, Sarah E., *Women in Classical Antiquity*, Pimlico Books, Random House, London

Ramachandran, V.S. and Blakeslee, S., *Phantoms of the Brain: Human Nature and the Architecture of the Mind*, Fourth Estate, London, 1998

Reeves, Paula, M., *Women's Intuition: Unlocking the Wisdom of the Body*, Conari Press, California, 1999

Robbins, Tom, *Still Life with Woodpeckers*, Corgi, London, 1980

Sabini, Meredith, 'Imagery in dreams of illness', *Quadrant*, Spring, 1982

Sabrin, T.R. and Juhasz, J.B., 'The social psychology of hallucinations', *Journal of Mental Imagery*, 2, 1978, 117–44

Serois-Berliss, Michelle and de Koninck, Joseph, 'Menstrual stress and dreams: adaptation or interference', *Psychiatric Journal of the University of Ottowa*, 7 (2), 1982

Sheldrake, Peter and Cormack, M., 'Dream recall and the menstrual cycle', *Journal of Psychosomatic Research*, 18, 1974

Shuttle, P. and Redgrave, P., *The Wise Wound*, Penguin 1980

Siegel, Bernie, *Love, Medicine and Miracles*, Arrow Books, London, 1988

Siegel, Bernie, *Peace, Love and Healing*, Rider, London, 1982

Signell, Karen, *Dreams: The Wisdom of the Heart*, Bantam Books, New York

Silverbear, Marion, *Dream Vestibule*, PO Box 263, Ben Lomand, CA 95005, USA

Stevens, Anthony, *Private Myths: Dreams and Dreaming*, Penguin, Harmondsworth, 1996

Stickgold, Robert, 'Sleep: offline memory reprocessing', *Trends in Cognitive Sciences*, 2, 1998, 484

—— 'Perchance to dream', *New Scientist*, 25 September 1999

Stoughton-Hyde, Lilian, *Favourite Greek Myths*, D.C. Heath, London

Sundance Community Dream Journal, Sundance, PO Box 395, Virginia Beach, VA 23451, USA

Taylor, Allegra, *I Fly Out With Bright Feathers: The Quest of a Novice Healer*, Fontana/Collins, London, 1987

Ulanov, Ann Bestford, *The Feminine in Jungian Psychology and in Christian Theology*, Northwestern University Press, Evanston, 1971

Ullman, M. and Zimmerman, N., *Working With Dreams*, Delacorte Press/Eleanor Friende, New York, 1979

Updike, John, *Self-Consciousness: Memoirs*, 1989, ch. 3.

van der Castle, Robert, *The Psychology of Dreaming*, General Learning Corporation, New York, 1971

Vann, B. and Alperstein, N., 'Dream sharing as a social interaction', *Dreaming*, 10 (2), 2000

Vaughan–Lee, Lweellyn, *Catching the Thread*, The Golden Sufi Center, California, 1998

Webb, W.B., *Sleep: The Gentle Giant*, Prentice Hall, N.J., 1975

Winget, C. and Kapp, F., 'The relationship of the manifest contents of dreams to the duration of childbirth in *prima gravidae*', *Psychosomatic Medicine*, 34 (2), 1972, 313–20

Woodman, Marion, *Bone: Dying Into Life*, Viking Penguin, New York, 2000

Woolger, Jennifer and Roger, *The Goddess Within*, Rider, London, 1990

Invitation

If you would like to contact me about your dreams I would be delighted to hear from you. I may not be able to reply to all queries but I will do my very best to help you.

As an author it is always a privilege to hear from readers, so do send me your comments on *Venus Dreaming* and details of dreams which have been important in your life.

May your dreams guide you on your path,
Brenda

Contact me at:

7 Didsbury Park
Didsbury
Manchester M20 5LH
England
email: lapwing@gn.apc.org

Brenda Mallon offers one-to-one dream work, runs dream groups and workshops. If you want further details please contact her at the above address.